Cultural Identity and Dalit Literature
Emergence of Madigas in Indian Society

Cultural Identity and Dalit Literature
Emergence of Madigas in Indian Society

Darla Venkateswara Rao
J. Bheemaiah

Prestige Books International
New Delhi

Published by
Prestige Books International
New Delhi 110 060
prestigebooks@gmail.com
Phone: 9818755529, 9810323134

Associate Office
Sydney 2001

ISBN: 978-81-947512-4-3

Printed in India

Contents

Preface
7

Part I
Madiga Identity in Modern Telugu Literature

Madiga Roots
15

Madiga in Telugu Literature
25

Subverting the Negative Images
44

Part II
Social, Cultural and Religious Perspectives

Tanning and Drumming as Cultural Identity
53

Ethnic Culture and Tradition:
A Comparative Reading of Igbo and Madiga
64

Valmiki's *Joothan* and Jashua's *Naakatha*
as Narratives of Lived Experiences
75

Dissenting Religious Fascism in Enoch's *Munivahanudu*
85

Bibliography
102

Preface

Metaphysics of *Jambapurana*

Ancient India was treasured with puranic literature which is a potential source of Indian culture and religion. These mythological texts narrate the history of the Universe ranging from creation to destruction. Cultural and literary texts also have preserved the genealogies of kings, heroes, sages, and deities. It is said that *puranas* are eighteen in number authored by Vyasa Maharshi in order to create bhakti and devotion among the masses. They have been under Brahminical dominance for centuries. This puranic literature had evolved as a special branch for persuasion by 600-300 A.D. The puranic literature underwent several changes. The educated elite from the dominant upper caste community had an opportunity to make changes to the line of their lineage. The lower castes had no role in this intellectual exercise. The fact that the people of the lower order were denied education for centuries. However, they continued to narrate their caste myth. In the beginning, all myths were narrated in Sanskrit language.

Sanskrit language was an impeccable medium of the Hindu religious texts. In fact, it was not a language of the common people. Sanskrit was considered as a divine language that served the elitist society. Ironically, the Hindu texts were meant to spread cultural devotion among the common masses. The ritualistic performances carried out by the Kings and Emperors of the day were recorded in puranas. Common people were not associated with puranas. Therefore, in line with the tradition, lower sections of society began to attribute the line of their descent to some purana or the other. In this backdrop, *Jambapurana* which emerged as a cultural magnum opus of the lower castes significantly traces the cultural roots of Madigas. Historians identified them as a tribe, and their self-respect was established through mythical stories of Arundhati and Kamadhenu.

It is an accepted fact that the practice of untouchability has been in India for centuries in one form or the other. Though India has reached its heights in technology and science, caste system still plays a major part in social, political and cultural life. Our nation is a haven for thousands of castes, sub-castes and dependent castes. Each caste has its socio-cultural lineage. Madiga is one of the principal sub-castes among the Dalits in India. Madigas are also known as Chamars in north India.

Jambapurana is a caste myth which is a source of Madiga culture and life. Given the cultural roots of Madiga, a sub-caste is distinguished from other innumerable sub-castes within the Dalit community for many reasons. Animal skin is a sort of material which was meant for human purpose in history.

Madiga or Chamar in India

Animal hides are utilized in many ways. Leather, a post-tanned material, has been associated with human needs for centuries. It has an inexhaustible relationship from the primitive man to the modern human being. There were successive changes in life with the discovery of animal skin, which became an essential need in human life. Tanners and leather workers are those who clean the animal raw hides for different purposes. In the primitive stage, leather was used as clothes for protection while skin was used as a mat. Tanners and leather workers are everywhere in the country and the world as well. But, they are differently designated as Chamars in the north and Madigas in the southern part of India. They have carved a niche in their contribution to Indian literature.

Madigas are known as descendants of Jambavanta or Jambavan in *Ramayana, Mahabharata and Bhagavatham*, the sources of Indian literature. Jamba Purana is the source to understand Jambavanta, the legendary figure of Madiga community. He was a Balluka King who was born from the yawn of Brahma. There is a reference of Jambavanta right from the Krita *Yuga* to the *Dwapara Yuga* (From Krita to Dwapara era). Jambavanta was alive when the churning of the ocean took place. He lived during the incarnation of Vamana. In *Ramayana*, he fought with Krishna from Rama's side. However, a Shamantakamani is offered to Krishna.

Both in Sundarakanda and Yuddha Kanda, Jambavanta often appears as elderly, prudent and strong. All others were unable to think as to how one would cross the ocean in an attempt to trace Sita. It is he who suggested that Hanuman was capable of tracing Sita. A demon called Saranu tells Ravana about Jambavanta and his brother, Dumaru. He describes that Dumaru is the commander of Balluka Veeras, who resides on a peak called Rukshavanta. Another Balluka Veera who resembles a mountain is none other than

Jambavanta. In prowess, Jambavanta is greater than his brother. He is the greatest man among all commanders. He is mighty and powerful. He likes serving the elders very much. He wins several battles and gets several sops in recognition of his support in the Devasura battle.

When Rama, Laxmana and the monkey army go faint, Hanuman and Vibhishan start searching for those who survived from among the dead. Jambavanta finds that Hanuman, the son of Anjani, is alive. To Vibhishan's surprise, Jambavanta says that if Hanuman is alive, the entire monkey army (if dead) will be brought back to life. If anything happens against it, we are deemed to be dead though we are alive. Hanuman is equivalent to wind in speed and fire in prowess. So, he wants Hanuman to fetch herbal medicines like *mritasanjeevani*, *vishallyakarani*, *sawarnakarani* and *sandanakarani* from Oushadi, a mountain lying in the midst of the Himalayas.

Jambavanta is a staunch devotee who witnesses some of the ten incarnations of Mahavishnu such as Kurma, Vamana, Rama and Krishna. He moves around the earth several times. As per the wish of the goddesses, he dumps all kinds of herbs available on earth into the milky ocean while it is being churned. During the performance of Balichakravarthy's *yagna* and Mahavishnu's incarnation as Thrivikrama, and while Brahma's feet are washed with *suraganga* water, Jambavanta makes several circumferences for Thrivikrama. During Rama's incarnation, he accompanies Hanuman and Angada, the ape heroes, in search of Sita. When ape heroes are ready, *prayaropaveshaniki* Jambavanta approaches Hanuman and inspires him by telling Hanuman's birth story and other curses-like-gifts. Later, the entire monkey army faints to Indrajith's *brahmastra.* The unaffected Vibhishan, while sharing with ape heroes the words of bravery, Hanuman too rises up and tries to make his monkey army enthusiastic. Then Vibhishan approaches Jambavanta and tells him. "Grandpa! I cannot see you because of the effect of *brahmastra.* I can identify you with your voice". Jambavanta asks Vibhishan, "Is the son of the wind safe?" With a surprise, Vibhishan replies to Jambavanta, "Grandpa! Why are you asking about Hanuman alone and why not Rama, Laxmana, Angada and Sugreeva? Does everything go auspicious only with Hanuman? It is his conviction towards Hanuman. Then Maruthi approaches Jambavanta and embraces him. Jambavanta asks him to fetch herbs from the mountain, the *Himagiri* to bring back the life of those who are fainted to the effect of *brahmastra.* There is a reference of Jambavanta even in the incarnation process of Krishna. Jambavanta not only fights with Krishna but also offers his daughter in marriage. Jambavanta is popular in Indian mythology and legends. His descendants have inherited a purana called *Jambapurana.*

Jambapurana is a representative text that signifies Jambavantas and extols their culture. Therefore, Jambavanta is a primordial Madiga. It can be presumed that Madigas who were said to be affluent in the remote past became impoverished because of their unselfish leather services rendered free of cost in order to serve the society. Madiga literature is being produced with the spirit of *Jambapurana.* In several states of India, some Madigas within the community still continue their ancestral caste-based occupation such as skinning and tanning. Thus, they carry a blemish of pollution/dirt attributable to untouchability.

Drumming for the upper castes on the festive occasions, shoe-making, fulfillment of leather needs for agriculture are associated with animal hides. Leather services of Madigas in rural India are highly significant and relevant even today.

There are innumerable sub-castes lying at the bottom within the Dalit community. Dalit by its origin is an umbrella term which accommodates several oppressed castes and sub-castes. Social life and culture of all the sub-castes are not the same. It varies from sub-caste to sub-caste. So Madiga culture is distinguished from that of the other Dalit sub-castes. Dalit intellectuals claim that Dalit literature is the literature of the oppressed produced by the Dalits themselves on caste lines and social predicament. Madiga writing is considered an important segment of Dalit literature. In fact, Dalit literature has emerged with the Madiga life as its centre.

Dalit literature includes caste oppression too. Apart from degradation of caste, other factors such as economic deprivation, defilement associated with skinning and tannings have historically projected Madigas as untouchables. Culture which evolved from their ancestral caste-based occupation has defined their social life. In fact, Madiga life is different from that of other Dalit individuals within the community. Madiga intellectuals have identified the Madiga community as a different sub-caste segment given its specific culture and literature. Madiga community has its dependent castes like Dakkali, Baindla, Chindu etc. Artistes of the dependent castes tend to eulogize Madiga ancestry, culture and its origin through their narrative performances. Given the changing lifestyles, most of the dependent castes of the younger generation are pursuing different occupations unrelated to their caste. Socio-economic and cultural gradations are deep rooted in *Varna.* Various sub-castes still practice cultural social and gradation. However, Jamba Purana, the source text of Madiga culture, is as relevant and equal as any other Indian purana.

A lot of poetry has been written glorifying the process of tanning, leather working and drumming by Madigas. Even non-Dalit writers have reflected the Madiga life and culture in different literary genres such as poetry, short fiction, novel and plays. Kolakaluri Enoch's *Munivahanudu* is a rare *Harijan* play that has been translated into several languages. It portrays the religious life of an Alvar of the lower community. In its decent portrayal, an upper caste priest who rejects the entry of an untouchable ultimately is bound to carry on his shoulder into the inner sanctum of the god. It is inevitable for the priest to bow down his head to the direction of the god. The act of carrying the untouchable devotee enlightens the priest. This even implies that temple is not built for the god alone but for the devotees too, who might be hailing from different quarters of society. They are all equal before God.

Whether oppressed sections believe 'in God or not' is not important but their entry into temples on par with other Hindu castes is important and relevant. Temple is considered as a site of social boycott because of caste. Madigas and other oppressed sections have demanded for temple entry. In the Indian reformation movement, social reformists placed the temple entry for Dalits as a main demand. Kolakaluri Enoch's *Munivahanudu* is a strong case in point. Several writings including poetry, short stories, and novels have been produced in favour of temple entry for all the Dalits. Of course, it is not just the problem of Madigas alone. It is the problem of all other Dalits who have been subject to caste discrimination in India for centuries together. *Jambapurana* stands as a response to both those who recognize caste as an identity, and to those who comment against the existing culture of the lowly. The so-called untouchables have tried to spread their cultural nobility through *Jambapurana* which finds a very significant place in Indian literature.

Hyderabad

Darla Venkateswara Rao
J. Bheemaiah

NOTE

1. The term' harijan' was used by Gandhiji in place of Aspurshya or antyaja as a reformatory measure of nomenclature before Independence. Kolakaluri continues the same in his drama.

Madiga Roots

Puranas have got a unique place in Indian Literature. Elitist Indians and their rulers as well claimed the greatness of their dynasty based on literary documents. This tradition continued to be reflected even in Telugu literature. No other puranas have as much significance as the eighteen puranas have in Telugu literary domain. Some puranas of the lower order continue to exist outside the chaturvarna frame. One of them is called *Jambapurana.*[1] Madigas are made part of panchamas who lived outside the Varna, a four-fold system of caste. Jamba-purana portrays the culture and life of Madigas. Great writers and critics argue and theorize that *Jambapurana* is also as great and equal as the eighteen Indian puranas. They attempted to delineate the cultural history and caste myth of Madigas.

Defining Purana

Researchers argue that *Astadasha puranas* and *Upapuranas* were written by Vyasa. But these legends have undergone a sea change with the passage of time. "According to *Apastamba Dharma Sutras,* puranic literature had evolved as a special branch by 600-300 A.D, which conformed to the teachings of the preachers. It underwent several changes until 12th century A.D." (Rao 4). It is understood that the educated elite section had an opportunity to make changes to the line of their lineage. Those who had been denied education for centuries continued to orally narrate their caste myth. So, the language used in puranas could not figure in the myth of the lower castes. The kings used to facilitate the glorification and valorization of lineage during the performances of rituals. It became a matter of prestige for the kings to have their descent recorded in the puranas. It became a tradition of the people of different sections to attribute the line of their descent to some purana or the other. Brahmins didn't tolerate the tall claim of the lower castes about their lineage. They separated the *Jambapurana* from the eighteen puranas labeling it a caste-myth. In fact, the structure of the eighteen puranas is the same as that of Kula Puranas or caste myths. According to the preface to Kurmapurana, purana is constituted mainly with the five salient features such as *sarga, prati sarga, lineage, Manvantara* and history of lineages.

> *Sagamu* is one that expands the entire world.
> *Prati sarga*: it connotes destruction.
> *Vamsam*: it is an interpretation on the production of lineage
> *Manvantara*: it acknowledges the happenings during the Manu period.
> *Wamsala Caritra*: history of lineages.

According to the *Bhagavata*, a purana should have ten attributes that include *Sargam* (creation), *Prati* Sarga (Calamity), *Vrithi* (Business), *Antaram* (the Manu period), *Wamsam* (About descendants), *Vamsanucaritam* (Narratives of Surya and Chandra descendants), *Samstha* (State), *Hethuvu* (cause), *Apasrayamu.* Puranas have been categorized into two kinds. Mahapuranas are those which have ten traits while those having five traits are called puranas (Rao 54). Researchers are of the view that *Jambapurana* is accepted as one among the Telugu folk arts. But the classical writers have not recognized it as one among the Ashtadasa Puranas (the eighteen legends) of India. Those who followed Sanskrit puranas, accepted them as standard texts but condemned all other folk traditional puranas. They dismissed them as fictitious. No history was created out of it. Hence its standardization is determined on belief; each purana has its own standardization. "If Kula Puranas are dismissed as fictitious and considered as imaginative, all other puranas are to be equally fictitious and imaginative in its logical sense. In fact, it is the Hindu ideological role that played behind this conspiracy" (Chary n.p).

Madiga Roots

Madiga literature revolves around the *Jambapurana* which is a potential source of culture and history of Madigas. The upper castes always tend to valorize their caste. In the same way, Madigas also try to emulate the upper castes in their caste identity and culture. Significantly, *Jambapurana* portrays self-respect of Madigas and their socio-cultural life. "Madigas were the rulers of various kingdoms in the ancient period. They became slaves after they were conquered in the war with the Aryans"(Babu 6). In this purana, the literary debate on the Madiga-Brahmana relationship continues at its philosophical level. There is a myth about Jambavamuni or Jambavanta that he was born before the creation itself and later the birth of Adishakti, Trinities, Kamadhenu, Saraswathi, Lakshimi and Parvathi took place. Naamalakanti Jagannatham who heralded the Madiga literature through the epics is of the view that there was no caste system in India but in the later period, it was imposed on Vashista and Arundathi (47). Dalit movements which demanded for equal rights came as a response to the Chanakya moral adopted by the upper castes in their clever tactics against vulnerable sections. Talluri Labun Babu in his book *Madiga Vari Charitra* (2001) mentions that "Jambavas were Madigas. They ruled ancient India which was known as Jambudweepam. Jambava was not the name of a person but the name of the Madiga community as a whole. In fact, Adi-Jambavas were of Alastroid origin. They were prosperous and civilized (17).

Boyi Bheemanna (1911-2005), a noted Telugu Dalit poet and playwright argues in favour of the literature of Madigas in his play *Raagavaashistam* which is considered the first legendary text.[2] Though Bheemanna was a Mala by caste, in the beginning, he wrote about the Mala-Madiga relation with the same outlook. He clarified it in the preface of his book. Based on the legendary theme, he wrote the love story of Vashista and Arundhati Devi who represent the Madiga community. "Madigas were the natives of the land and had lived prior to Brahmins. The Madiga community was mentioned as the first community. Even today, Madigas are frequently called 'upper caste' (Rao n.p).

It was the Maharshi Vyasa who was responsible for the birth of the Pandavas. Parashara was born to Sathyavathi, a Sudra woman. Brahmins monopolized the *Vedas* as their treasuries of knowledge. They revered Pandavas because of their noble birth. The author is of the view that "the caste hierarchy was determined based on the deed not on the Varna or birth. It was interpreted through *Guna-karma*[3] theory" (Nomulakanti 47). Caste Hindus are the firm believers of this theory. Kolakaluri Enoch narrates the story of Thiruppan Alwar in his play *Munivahanudu* (A bearer of Muni, 1976) which explores life and devotion of Madigas. The entire story is enriched with the portrayal of Madiga culture and tradition. "Madigas were historically Jambavas. In ancient times, Kshatriyas ruled India. In fact, "Jambudweepam, the ancient India, belonged to Madigas" (Babu 2-6). He cites puranas as incontrovertible evidence to substantiate his argument that Jambavanta was not the name of a person but it was the Madiga community. In the primitive age, hides of animals were used to protect from chill. Madigas displayed dexterity in turning hides into the protective clothing in the process of tanning.

The life of Madigas defines their culture and social status in society. The way non-Madigas theorized in classical literature about the life of Madigas is hardly helpful to understand their true cultural life. Non-Madigas have failed to give a true picture of Madiga life. Caste Hindus are intended to discharge their duties within the Varna frame. In fact, all the occupations should get equal priority and dignity. But some are treated as low and some others as high. Why this inequality? The ancestral cultural legacy of Madigas clarifies that occupation of Madigas was as noble as that of anybody else. It is bound to prove when its history is properly studied from the perspective of the dignity of occupational work.

Madigas were the rulers of various kingdoms in ancient India. But they became *dasyu*[4] after being conquered by the Aryans. Gradually they became *dasas*"[5] (Babu 6). According to *Jambapurana,* Madigas who enjoyed an ideal social position in the past became Dasas due to the curse of gods. *Jambapurana* significantly traces how Madigas were made untouchables. "*Kamadhenu*[6] is the divine cow which can feed any number of people. Parvathi invites only gods, goddesses and sages to taste its milk and milk products. An adolescent who looks after *Kamadhenu* feels like tasting the cow's milk. When he expresses his desire to Parvathi, she asks him to go and tell Kamadhenu. On hearing the desire, the divine cow collapses and dies. All the gods and goddesses eagerly flock around it for its flesh. Jambavanta and Chennaiah, the boy, start cooking the flesh. While stirring it, a piece falls down from the vessel, the boy and Jamabavanta put it back into the vessel. For this act, they are cursed to be born as untouchables on earth. This story provides a mythical basis for self-esteem of Madigas" (Chandraiah 24).

Jambavanta as Primordial Madiga

Jambapurana and the stories of Arundhati provide incontrovertible evidence to substantiate the Madiga claim. *The Ramayana* and the *Bhagavata* inform that Rama and Krishna too had close relations with Jambavanta. It clarifies further that no other sub-caste in the Dalit community has such a great cultural legacy as the Madigas enjoyed. Jambavanta is said to be born as a bear from Brahma's yawn. There are innumerable references about him through *Kritha*[7] and *Dwapara yugas*.[8] He was not only present during the churning of the sea but also threw his presence during the incarnation of Vamana. He stood by Rama in wars. He married off his daughter, Jambavati to Krishna and also gifted him *Shyamantakamani*, a precious stone. Jambavanta is depicted as a prudent veteran in the episodes of

Sundarakanda[9] and *Yuddhakanda*[10] of *Ramayana.* When all were anxious about abducted Sita, he was the one who recommended the name of Hanuman for he was able to solve the problem. He was a wise person who was aware of the capabilities of Hanuman. It is construed that considering his merit, Jambavanta was inevitably given a space in the traditional *purana-itihasas.*[11]

Yendluri Sudhakar, a Telugu poet writes about Trinities who considered Jambavamuni as a low caste. It is constructed from '*Aaran Jyothi*' as to how Brahmins treat Arundhati as an untouchable woman and kill her with conspiracy. To hide their crime, they set her on marriage fire. "The Hindu married couple is mandated to look at the Arundhati star soon after marriage is performed. It is a kind of reverence shown to Arundhati. The story of Arundhati informs the significance of this custom (113-16). Some scholars are of the view that legendary stories and mythical concepts are exploited by the vested interests.

Janethihasas show evidence through some stories about these legends. One such story is connected with 'Vontimitta' which is the Mandal headquarter located 20 km away from Rajampet in Kadapa district of Andhra Pradesh. The 'Vontimitta temple' is popularly known as Ekasla Nagaram where the people believe that Jambavanta installed an idol in the Kodanda Rama temple. Madigas still keep worshipping the idols of Jambavanta as their revered primordial man throughout Andhra and Karnataka states. All this manifests the cultural legacy of Madigas. "*Jambapurana* ought to be understood as a parallel Dalit legend placed against the hegemony of savarna castes. It also proves that the caste of Madigas is greater than any other caste" (Lakshminarayana vi). Basically, Madigas are skilled people. *Jambapurana* stands as impeccable evidence of the occupational history of Madigas.

From Plenty to Poverty

History is constructed out of facts and fiction, essentially from fiction-centered kavyas, puranas and classic folk narratives. Though, at times, poetry is woven out of facts, its fictitious creation is equally significant. When we critically look at the present economic scenario of Madigas, we understand that curse is the reason for their misery. But it appears to be far from the truth. Probably, their livelihood was better despite the fact that they were involved in the traditional occupation of skinning dead animals from the beginning. They never spent their life without work. They were only the people who fulfilled leather related agricultural needs of the villagers. They could create abundant employment opportunities in their own village. In fact, they suffered no scarcity of food. They prioritized and dedicated their occupation to serve the society rather than marketing it for money. So, they faced a binary problem. In the name of social service, they offered leather goods free of cost, which became a tradition. Continuity of this tradition pushed them into poverty. Several other castes too faced this problem; but surprisingly only Madigas were driven into bonded-labour. Second, Madigas didn't think of migrating to other places for livelihood as they were solely depending upon their caste-based occupation in the village. They were struck with both poverty and illiteracy in the long run. Thus, they lost cultural glory of their past.

Conclusion

Jambapurana as a caste myth of Madigas has not been considered one among the Hindu puranas owing to the Brahmanical conspiracy which blurred its visibility as Mahapurana. Jambavanta, the primordial cultural symbol of Madigas, is accepted into the Hindu epics under unavoidable circumstances given his prudence and gallantry in times of trouble. *Jambapurana*, a cultural magnum opus, traces the roots of Madigas and their self-respect through mythical stories of Arundhati and Kamadhenu. Madigas attribute the social practice of untouchability to the curse of gods and goddesses. It can be presumed that Madigas who were affluent in the ancient past became impoverished because of their unselfish leather services rendered free of cost in order to serve the Indian society. Madiga literature is being produced with the spirit of *Jambapurana*.

NOTES

1. *Jambapurana* belongs to the Madiga community. It is a caste myth which interprets the Madiga culture and its social life. It is the sloka that Sutha preached to the Rishis all eight puranas while satrayaga was going on. It is mentioned in the first *skandha* of Bhagavata Purana. Madwayam Bhadwayam chaiva bratrayam, Vachatustayam Anaapadingakuskani puranani *pruthak:*
   From the above:
   'Ma' dwayam--Mashyapuranam, Markandeyapuranam
   "Bha" dwayam--Bhagavata Purana, Bhavishya Puranam.
   "Bra" trayam--Brahma Puranam, Brahma Vaivarta Puranam, Brahmanda Puranam.
   "Va"-Chatustayam--Vishnu Puranam, Varaha Puranam, Vaamanapuranam, Vayu Puranam.
   Foot of the sloka is composed with the first letter of other puranas.

Agni Puranam
Na-Narada Puranam
Pad-Padma Puranam
Lim-Lingapuranam
Ga-Garudapuranam
Ku-Kamapuranam
Ska-Skanda Purana
Slokas are taken from Astadasa Puranam.

2. *Raagavasistam*. http://eemaata.com/em/issues/200809/1317.html
3. Gunas are the character or qualities that govern our nature and behaviour. Karma, a Sanskrit word that roughly translates to "action," is a core concept in some Eastern religions, including Hinduism and Buddhism. Importantly, karma is wrapped up with the concept of reincarnation or rebirth, in which a person is born in a new human (or nonhuman) body after death.
4. Dasyu, Sanskrit dāsa ("servant"), an aboriginal people in India who were encountered by the Indo-European-speaking peoples who entered northern India about 1500 B.C.
5. Dasa, or das, also means a "servant of God", "devotee.
6. A miraculous cow of plenty who could give her owner whatever he desired. Kamadhenu appeared on earth as one of the precious things that were brought to light in the Churning of the Ocean.
7. The *Krita Yuga* lasts 4,000 years, with a dawn and dusk of 400 years each, for a total of 4,800 years..
8. *Dwapara Yuga*, is the third out of four Yugas, or ages, described in the scriptures of Hinduism.
9. Sundarakanda is the fifth book in the Hindu epic, the Ramayana. The work depicts the adventures of Hanuman and his selflessness, strength, and devotion to Rama are emphasized in the text. Hanuman was fondly called "Sundara" by his mother Anjani and Sage Valmiki chose this name over others as the Sundara Kanda is about Hanuman's journey to Lanka.
10. Yuddha Kandam is a single but long chapter in Adhyatma Ramayanam. Rama and his friends decide to go to Lanka, cross the ocean and bring back Sita.
11. Purana is the narration of incidents that occurred in the remote past while itihasa is the epic which is the narration of incidents that occurred during the lifetime of the narrator.

Madiga in Telugu Literature

Telugu literature has about fifteen hundred years of history. In the 11th century, Nannayya authored the *Andhra Mahabharata*. He was the court poet during the reign of Raja Narendra and he wrote this seminal book only to protect the *Varnashrama Dharma* (caste-based duties).[1] It was the sole duty of the rulers of ancient India to protect the Varnashrama Dharma. These Varnashrama Dharma were evolved based on the *Manusmriti* and other Hindu *Shastras*.[2] The ancient poets treated the Madigas as Sudras through the interpretation of *Varnashrama Dharma*. *Manusmriti* makes it clear that it is a virtuous duty of the Sudras to serve the Brahmins, Kshatriyas and Vaishyas (the three upper castes in the Hindu caste pyramid) without any prejudice. This would be an ideological extension in the ancient Telugu literature. The modern literature portrays the life of Madigas from the human perspective, which is entirely different in its interpretation from that of the ancient literature. So, the problem of caste is discussed based on the mythological, ancient and modern interpretations.

Madiga as Social Category

The Indian constitution has listed different races and castes as Scheduled Castes and Scheduled Tribes. Madiga is one of the 62 sub-castes under Scheduled Caste category in two Telugu states. However, the Malas and Madigas are technically untouchables but culturally they are different from each other. Other sub-castes within the Dalit community continue to remain frontal to these main castes. The same is carried into Telugu literature too. The Mala-Madiga castes were termed in different nomenclatures such as *Aspurushyas, Chandalas, Panchamas and Harijans.* Dr. Ambedkar was opposed to these Sanskrit terms and he replaced them with Depressed Classes and Protestant Hindus. The term, Dalit, was recently coined 'which means social misery, broken people and oppressed sections of India. Now, the untouchables are familiar socially, politically and academically as Dalits. In literature, Madigas are clearly identified based on their culture. Madigas were involved in skinning the cattle, eating beef, tanning, making leather shoes, drum-beating on specific occasions for generations (Kancha Ilaiah 1996: iii).

Madiga in Dictionaries

In dictionaries, the term 'Dalit' would mean caste. Madiga sub-castes include Jambavas, Arundhati Yas, Gosangas, Chandalas, Baindlas, Kommulas, Mathangas and Pambalas etc. In ancient Telugu literature, Madigas were not distinguished from Malas in terms of social and cultural life. In the light of the sub-caste classification, Madigas have been depicted with their cultural identity in modern Telugu literature.

Madiga in Puranas

Jambapurana foregrounds the 'self-respect' of Madigas from a different perspective. The debate on the Madiga-Brahmana relationship takes place at a philosophical level in this purana. According to the *Jambapurana,* Jambavamuni was born before the creation per se. Adhishakti, Trinities, Kamadhenu, Saraswathi, Lakshimi and Parvathi were born next to him. Researchers opine that *Jambapurana* is one among the disciplines of the Telugu folk arts. The classical writers have not recognized it as one of the *ashtadasa puranas* (Eighteen legends) of India. It is based on the Hindu ideology. However, *Jambapurana* gives an inspiration to the emergence of the Madiga literature.

Based the cultural history, Madigas tend to glorify and emulate the upper castes in terms of caste status in society. Thus, they ennoble their own caste. *Raagavaashistam* (love bond of Vashista: 1959), the first legendary–social play written by Boyi Bheemanna argues in favour of the Madiga literature. Though Bheemanna was a Mala by caste, he writes about the Mala-Madiga relation with a unified outlook which is discernable in the preface to his play. Based on the legendary theme, he portrays the love story of Vashista and Arundhati Devi. Arundati represents the Madiga women. Namalakanti Jagannatham's Arundhati *Devi Charitramu* (history of Arundhati Devi-1968), argues that the history of Madigas was noble and there was no caste system at all. But in the later period, a certain caste was attributed to Vashista and Arundhati (1968:47). Namalakanti heralds a new literary trend in the Madiga literature with reference to Sanskrit and Telugu Mahabharata, Bhagavata, the Ramayana and puranas. It is said that Maharshi Vyasa was responsible for the birth of Pandavas. Parashara was born to Sathyavathi, a Sudra woman. Brahmins treated the Vedas as their own treasuries of knowledge, which were actually **sorted** out to their order by Parashara. They respected and valorized the Pandavas because they were not born low. The writer is of the view that caste differences were maintained based on one's deeds not on Varna (1968:47). He also authored the book titled *Arundhati Yula Vamshavriksham* (Chronological History of Arundhati Yas). Nallapati Shivanaraiah's articles with citations from the Hindu mythology argue in support of the Madiga literature. His articles provide a basis for the idea of the Madiga culture and history.

Kolakaluri Enoch, in his play *Munivahanudu* (1976: A Bearer of Muni-), narrates the story of Thiruppan Alwar. The story depicts the devotional life of Madigas. B.V.S Murthy in his book *Kathamanjari* (1992) writes the stories about Madigas and other untouchables. The book delineates not only the story of a devotee called Lakshimamma who belongs to the Mathangi caste but also deals with *Arundhati Devi Charitra* (1992:111-18). Bonigala Rama Rao's *Mala-Madigala Cheritra* (1997: the History of Mala-Madigas) emphasizes with reference to *Jambapurana* that Madigas were created prior to Brahmins. Madiga is mentioned as the first community. S.T. Gnanada Kavi, in his book *Scheduled Kulalu Antaraniwara?* (1997) (Scheduled Castes: Untouchables?), argues that Madigas were considered the noble people in history. He strengthens his viewpoint based on the stories and references drawn from the puranas. Talluri Laban Babu argues in *Madiga Charitra* (1998: The Madiga History) from a new perspective. He is of the view that Madigas were Jambavas and they belonged to the Kshatriyas community which ruled India in the ancient times. He also says that Jambudwipam was a country which belonged to Madigas (2002:2-6). Based on the puranas, he strengthens his argument that Jambavanta is not the name of a person but it is the name of the Madiga community. Animal hides were used to protect from chill. Madigas, who displayed expertise in turning animal hides into protective clothing, were called tanners.

Talluri's book scientifically analyses the living ways of Madigas. He writes his book from the perspectives of anthropology, history and puranas. In *Ekalavya*, Kancha Ilaiah interprets the dimensions of the Madiga purana from the economic perspective. He has published a booklet titled *Madiga Arthika Saangika Tatwam* (1996: Economic and Social Philosophy of Madigas). We can make out Chadala as Madiga from his conversation with Adishankaracharya. Bonigala Rama Rao mentions this fact in *Aadiguruvu Acharya Chandala* (Chandala-the first teacher: 2005). Yendluri Sudhakar narrates two legendary stories about the Madiga life in *Malle Moggala Godugu-Maadiga Kathalu* (The Umbrella Buds of Jasmine and the Madiga Narratives: 1999). In the story 'Jambavanta-Pachamama' (Jambavanta and Mad Uncle: 17-201), Yendluri Sudhakar writes about how the Trinities treat Jambavamuni as a low caste. From 'Aaranjyothi' (Arundhati Devi: 113-16), it is understood that Brahmins consider Arundhati as a low caste woman and they conspire to kill her. To hide their crime, they set her on marriage fire. Yendluri argues that the story of Arundhati lies behind this cruel custom. The Hindu married couple is mandated to have a glimpse of the Arundhati star after marriage. It is a kind of veneration displayed to Arundhati. The rationalists feel that legendary stories and mythical concepts are meant for vested interests. Social imbalances, caste inequalities serve as a curse against the lower castes. Narla Venkateshwara Rao, one of the rationalists, castigated the puranas. With reference to *Puranas- Kula Vyavastha*

(Legends and Caste System: 2001, 2003: Hyderabad book Trust), B. Vijaya Bharathi says that "if any person believes in the *Ashtadasa Puranas*, he/she should also equally believe in *Jambapurana* too". She continues to ennoble the life of Madigas through the legendary literature. Her statement exemplifies it.

Madigas in Ancient Telugu Literature

In ancient Telugu literature, Madigas are referred to as Sudras and Chandalas. Among Shaiva poets, Palkuri Somanatha (12th century), a Madiga bhakta, wrote a story titled *Bogaiah gari Katha.* Sri Krishna Devaraya (16th century) also wrote a book called *Mala Dasari Katha.* Though he mentions 'Mala' in his story, the term implies Chandala. Vemana (17th century) also comments on Madigas and praises Arundathi. Gurujada Appa Rao (19th century), in his *Lavana Raju Katha*, says, "if the good is Mala, I shall become a Mala'. Here Mala is considered an untouchable.

As far as Telugu literature is concerned, the literary contribution from the 11th century to 19th century was made from the view point of the Varna system. Though Veerashaivas, Brahma Naidu and Vemana were opposed to the Varna system, they could not influence Telugu literature. He was a Brahmin who wrote *Mala Dasari Katha* in the 16th century. When critics look at it in devotional terms, Mala Dasari seems to have been portrayed as noble. From the view point of the Varna system, Sri Krishna Devaraya, depicts Mala as an untouchable. The devotion of a lower caste man was felt necessary to redeem the upper caste man. But the devotion was not considered as an accepted norm for temple entry. Palkuriki Somanatha tells about it in *Basava Purana*. In *Bogaiah Katha*, Shiva comes to Bogaiah's house in guise and asks him to cook the flesh of a cow for him. Bogaiah cooks it. Brahmins come to know this and assault him. They suspect that he would pollute Agraharam, the village. Because of this troubling situation, Bogaiah leaves the village declaring that he will not depend on Agraharam for his livelihood. The entire village becomes disintegrated. In the face of the disturbing developments, Brahmins call Bogaiah back and treat him with respect.

Mangipudi Venkata Sharma (20th century) claims in *Nirudda Bharatham* that Madigas belong to the dynasty of Mathanga Mahamuni. It is Joshua (20th century), the poet, who depicts Madigas for the first time in Telugu poetry. He himself says that he belongs to the Madiga caste. But he frequently uses the term 'Harijan' in his poetry. He demands the eradication of untouchability under the aegis of Gandhiji. His *Gabbilam* (The Bat) is a great poem which depicts the agony of Dalits.

Yendluri Sudhakar has written poetry from the perspective of the Madiga self-identity. He feels that Scheduled Caste reservations should reach out not only to the Mala-Madigas but also to all the 62 sub-castes under the Scheduled Caste Category. He wrote "Dakkali Pilla" in Andhra Prabha daily dated 06-09-1998 with an appeal to the Madigas that they should give the Dakkalis their legitimate share from the reservation benefits in a similar way that Madigas demand their genuine share of reservation from Malas.

> We had at least a hut for our heads
> Under the roof of the sky

The girl wandered like a nomad. (Darky, 2002, trans. MO)

Yendluri's "Dakkali Pilla" is an appeal for the legitimate share of reservations for Dakkalis in order to give them social upliftment. The poet sarcastically depicts that Madigas are enjoying the legitimate share of Dakkalis. In the same way Malas are infringing upon the rights of Madigas. This indicates that one dominant sub-caste caste exploits the other sub-caste. He brings out the facts on how reservation is being misused by the sub-castes within.

In "Dasunu Chudali" (I want to see Dasu), Yendluri also argues that Malas and Madigas share similar miseries. Though they mingled one another and lived happily in the past, they have become like worn out shoes, and they could not be united. The poem foregrounds that though Malas and Madigas equally suffer the malady of untouchability, they are distinct from each other in terms of cultural life. There is a rift between the two categories due to the fact that Madigas demand the legitimate share in the constitutional benefits in proportion to their population. But Malas are exploiting the major share against their population. In fact, Madiga population is more than Mala population. The poem wonderfully depicts the mental attitude of Malas and Madigas who have been temporarily parted from each other due to this problem.

Yendluri justifies his demand for constitutional justice through his literary writing.

Madiga in Modern Telugu Poetry

Dalit poetry has secured a distinct place in the domain of Telugu literature. Madiga poetry mainly focuses on the contemporary social movements. With the emergence of Madiga Dandora Movement, Madiga poetry has reached its zenith and Madigas started writing poetry on various social issues. Yendluri Sudhakar tops among the Madiga poets. Yendluri has written "Vargikaraneeyam" (2003: Classification), "Kottagabilam" (1998: New Bat), "Nalla Drakhsa Pandiri" (2002: Darky) to his credit. He is successful in the representation of the Madiga issues in his two long poems. *Madiga Chaitannyam* (1997: Madiga Consciousness), an anthology of poetry, published by Madiga Sahitya Vedika is said to be the first anthology of poetry. In this, Madigas themselves wrote poems and songs highlighting their problems. The anthology which consists of the literary contributions of the eminent poets also includes Yendluri Sudhakar's *Dasunu Chudali*,(I want see Dasu).Kolakaluri Enoch's *Cheppulaku Namaskaristhunnanu* (I Greet the Foot-Wear), Nagappagari Sundara Raju's *Madigodu* (A Madiga), Darla Venkateshwara Rao's *Madiga Manifesto*, Katti Kallyan Chandra's *Uniki* (Existence) etc. This anthology has twenty three poems which include M. Johnson's *Madiga Chaitanyam*,(the Madiga Conscious) Ravinuthula Prem Kishire's *Dandora*, Vijaya Rathnam's *Madiga Mahathu*, Anand's *Yellamma Jatara*, (the Yellamma Festival), *Kashi Madiga's Roadumeeda Dandora* (Dandora on the Road), Tudi Mahender's *Madiga Jeevitham* (the Madiga life), Kolluri Chiranjeev's *Nenumadigonni* (I am the Madiga), Chitram Prasad's *Chatimpu* (the Announcement), Ashavadi Shashanka Mouli's *Peddintolla Shweta Patram* (the White Paper of the Big House), Vemula Yellaiah's *Katti Arini Padunupeduthunnam,* Kolakaluri Srinivasa Rao's *Tera Dinchutam* (We Down the Curtain), Rajalingam's *Oh Madiga Uddyaminchu* (Oh Madiga Agitate), Talluri Basupratap's *Ahavaninchu* (Invite) Masterji's *Evaranukunnaru* (Who do you think?) etc.

Nagappagari Sunder Raju has published an anthology of poetry titled *Chandala Chatimpu* (1996), Gyara Yadaiah discusses the significance of Madiga culture in his anthologies of poetry *Gutam Debba and Erkopi*. Ravinuthala Prem Kishore has written a long poem titled "Gunde Daruvu" (2000). Several Madigas are writing their poetry separately.

Critics have accepted the Madiga poetry with its significance on social issues. G. Lakksmi Narasaiah, an eminent critic (1995-65) is of the view that Madiga poetry established a new trend in Dalit poetry and it is flourishing.

Madiga Poetry

Madiga poetry is written against the caste-based discrimination. It expresses the fact that 'giving a clarion call for unity among Mala-Madigas is all humbug'. Madiga poetry protects Madiga rights and protests against those who infringe upon its legitimate rights. It is unique in its history and culture. Madiga poetry depicts the true Ambedkarism. It evolved from the ideology Baba Saheb Ambedkar. The main thrust of this poetry is to demand equal rights to the Dalits (to all the sub-castes). It makes clear that untouchability exists even among untouchables. There is hierarchy within the community. Madiga poetry is neither intended to split Dalits nor it is meant to create inimical contradictions among them but it tries to negotiate with the past and demands proper distribution of constitutional benefits among all sub-castes. This does not mean to destabilize the unity. When Madiga poetry began to be produced, all other oppressed sections also started writing poetry reflecting their problems. Madiga poetry inspired Tribes and other Backward Class people who started discussing their socio-culture issues. It plays a key role in the creation of social awareness among all the oppressed sections of society.

Madiga poetry valorizes the traditional occupation and protects its cultural nobility. It has introduced its terminology to create its own aesthetics in literary writing. Thus, it adds a new vocabulary to the Telugu language. Jupaka Subadra, Gogu Shyamala, Jajula Gouri, among all others people are writing Madiga poetry from a new perspective. The sentiments of the Telangana people are truly reflected in their poetry. Malas too started writing against the Madiga poetry with a voice of unity among Dalits. Satish Chandra, Paidi Terish Babu, Gutam Swami are among those who are opposed to the Madiga poetry. They don't want to consider it as Dalit literature.

Most of the Dalit poets used to condemn every ignoble deed of the upper castes in their poetry. They have started writing from the sub-caste perspective in the post Dandora movement. Dalit poets like Katti Padma Rao and Shikhamani have not reflected in their poetry about the essence of the Dandora Movement which has been demanding the classification of the Scheduled Castes. Dalit poets are not interested to expose the internal disparities among the Dalits. This smacks of discrimination within the community. They have nourished antagonistic attitudes towards Madiga poetry.

Narratives

Sripada Subramanyam's "Pullam Raju Katha" (A Story of Pullam Raju) which was written for the first time, delineates the life of Madigas. Later, he wrote stories like

"Sagarasangamam" (1931: Convergence of the River); *Madiga Palle* (The Madiga Ghetto): "Ilaanti Tavvaai Vasthe" (1934: If the Way is Like this). The story focuses on disunity, cultural differences and economic disparities among Dalits. It also portrays how the upper castes dominate and exploit the lower castes taking advantage of their disunity and poverty. Gopi Chand, in his story, "Cheppulu Kuttevadu" (1961: Shoe Maker) depicts the life of the Madiga shoemakers. He also describes how miserably they are dying of dust in their lungs. In their occupation, they are exposed to dust on the open roads.

Kolakaluri Enoch's long story "Urabavi" (The Public Well) depicts the problem of drinking water in the village. It also illustrates the adventure of a Madiga woman who rebels against the atrocities of the dominant upper castes. The story is told with a Chanakya moral. The woman champions the cause of the lower order. G. Bhanu in his "Paapaniki Jeetham" (1969: Return for the Sin) portrays how Madiga woman rebels against an upper caste landlord who attempts to force her into sex. He kills her because of her strong resistance. Finally, he dies of a terrible sore in his leg due to sin. Karma Theory is the crux of the story. In "Talli Matti" (1991: The Mother Soil), Swamy describes how the educated Madigas are caught in the inferiority complex, who hesitate to reveal their caste. In "Jeeva Nadulu" (1991: Assimilated Culture), Shanti Narayana foregrounds how the upper people do not want to attend the marriages of Madigas. Even Nayi Brahmnas are reluctant to play music for Madigas. Kaluva Mallaiah in his *Agnigundam* (1991: The Well of Fire) describes that Madigas are serving the society by drumming on various occasions of the village celebrations. Despite this, their services are no longer recognized. To overcome such predicament, they feel that education is only the weapon that would liberate their children. Upper castes conspire to implicate the Madiga children into false cases. Shanti Narayana, in his "Ukku Padam" (Iron Foot), delineates how a minister belonging to the Madiga community is unable to exercise his political power under the upper caste domination. The political office without economic power is given in name which is really of no use. The story underlines that without social equality, reservations alone would not benefit the Madigas.

In the light of the classification of reservation, several writers have exposed all kinds of disparities among Mala-Madigas. Tholeti Jaganmohan Rao's "Varnasrama", "Paidi" Terish Babu's "Anubandha Prashna" (the Affiliated Query), Sannapu Reddy Venkata Reddy's "Antu" (Pollution), Madduri Nagesh Babu's "Doma Tera" (The Mosquito Net), "Swamy's Prasthanam" (Journey) are some of the stories written on the issue of classification.

Kolakaluri Enoch has written several stories on Madigas from the Ambedkar perspective. His stories depict Madiga life in different perspectives. Among other stories, "Urabavi" (The Village Well), "Takattu" (Mortgage), "Godla Donga", "Kulavritti" and "Pottapegulib Bandigodu" are worth mentioning. In the story, "Takattu", Kolakaluri Enoch tries to delineate the true relationship between the Brahmin and the Madiga teachers.

In "Godla Donga" (Thief of the Cattle), Naagadu by name living on butchery is suspected to be responsible for the theft of the cattle in the village. Naagadu himself keeps a vigil throughout the night to catch the thief. He finds that the village upper caste head (Dora) resorts to the theft of the cattle. Dora is caught red-handed and is handed over to the villagers. He thinks that Dora will be surely let off. To avoid this, he kills him and inserts the dead body into the stomach of an ox and throws it into a gorge. The theft of the cattle stops ever since Dora disappears. Kolakaluri Enoch depicts how Doras (Dominant upper caste village heads) brand the Madigas as cattle thieves. "Pottapegulib Bandigodu" portrays that Dora grabs the land of Madigas taking advantage of their innocence and illiteracy. A Madiga youth kills Dora to get back his land. "Kula Vrutti" (2006: Caste Based Occupation) demands the traditional occupation of Madigas to be as equally noble as the traditional occupations of other castes in society. Kolakaluri Enoch is the one who occupies the first place among the story writers writing about Madigas on different social issues.

Yendluri Sudhakar has written "Mallemoggala Godugu Madiga Kathalu" (1999) which signifies and valorizes the Madiga life. In the story, he ennobles the Madiga occupation, culture and dialect. He portrays struggles and conflicts entwined in Madiga life from the time of puranas to the present day. Both Madiga and non-Madiga writers declare that for Madigas, shoes are regarded as equal to the goddesses. They depict the innate talent of Madigas who display it in their skinning and tanning. They have won accolades from the *Nawabs* (Lords) of that time. In the beginning, Christianity took care of Madigas; in the later period, caste discrimination and exploitation came into practice even in that religion. There are some stories which depict that liberation is possible only through Ambedkarism. Commenting on these stories, Lakshminarasaiah, an eminent critic, describes Yendluri Sudhakar as Madiga Gorky. Nagappagari Sunder Raju's story titled *Madigodu* (The Madiga Person) provides insights on the Madiga life and culture. Critics are of the view that the stories of Yendluri Sudhakar and Nagappagari Sunder Raju have introduced a genre of autobiography in Telugu Literature.

On the whole, several writers have produced stories depicting the Madiga life on varied themes. The stories are written out of sympathy and generosity by the non-Madiga writers to represent the issues of untouchability, denial of temple entry, and inter-caste marriages. They have hardly touched on the problem of conflict in Madiga life. The stories written by some upper caste writers depict that even the highly educated Madigas who sought government jobs by virtue of reservation, are not able to reveal their social category openly. For social equality, they tend to embrace religions other than Hindu religion. Kolakaluri Enoch, Yendluri Sudhakar, Boya Jangaiah, Nagappagari Sunder Raju, Gogu Shyamala, Jupaka Subadra and J. Gouri are those among the Madiga writers who strongly reflected the conflict of Madiga life in their stories.

Fiction

Non-Dalit writers too reflected the Dalit problem through their novels written in the 19th and 20th centuries. Some of them include Kandukuri Veeresalingam Panthulu's *Rajashekara Charitram* which is a social novel written in1878. The protagonist of the novel does not take water offered by an untouchable while *Rangaraja Cheritramu* (1872) written by Gopala Krishnama Shetty, depicts the story of a Kshatriya woman who grows in a *Girijana* family.

Talla Pragada Surya Narayana's *Helavathi* (1910) is the first Telugu novel which sympathetically portrays the problems of Mala-Madigas. There are some other novels like Unnava Lakshimi Narayanas's *Malapalli* (1921-22: Ghetto of Malas), Veluri Shivarama Sastri's *Obaiah* (1920), Ranganayakamma's *Balipeetam* (1953: Altar), Akkineni Kutunba Rao's *Sorajjam* (1981), Volga's *Akasamlo Sagam* (1990: A Half in the Sky), were written from the Mala-Madiga perspective.

Only after 1980s, the novels written by Dalit writers began to appear. They were written with Dalit consciousness. G Rama Mohan Rao's *Kakibathukulu* (1980-82: Lives of the Police) was written under his pen name, Spartacas. Sadananda Sharada's *Manchinilla Bavi* (1992: The Well of Drinking Water), Kaluva Mallaiah's *Gaddalu Tandayi* (1996), *Neebanchan Kalmokta* (1987: I am your Slave), *Sambaiah Chaduvu Bathuku Pusthakam*, Chilukuri Devaputra's *Panchamam* (1998: The Fifth Caste), P. Nasaraiah's *Madigapalle* (1998: Ghetto of Madigas), G. Kalyan Rao's *Antarani Vasantam* (2007: Untouchable Spring), Vemula Yellaiah's *Kakka* (2000), *Siddi* (2006), Gopararu Nageshwar Rao's *Dandemmeedi Chilukalu* (2001), Boyi Jangaiah's *Jatara* (1997:Festival), *Maromaarpu* (2002) delineate the social consciousness of the Mala-Madigas.

Vemula Yellaiah's *Kakka* portrays how the upper caste landlords create troubles for Madigas. In this novel, language, culture and traditions are discussed in detail. The novel has been translated into English and published recently. In Chilukuri Devaputra's *Panchamam* (The Fifth Caste), the protagonist, Shivaiah, belongs to the Madiga caste. His father is a drummer. Shivaiah who seeks higher education with the encouragement of an upper caste man, becomes a District officer. The dominant upper caste ministers want to ensure that Sivaiah does not implement land reforms in the Revenue Department. When Sivaiah does not cooperate with the ministers, they get him suspended on charge of accepting bribes. Even the Deputy Chief Minister belonging to Madiga caste is unable to protect Sivaiah. The novel manifests that though higher positions are offered by virtue of reservation, political offices/powers cannot uplift the Madigas. In this novel, social reality of fifty years of Dalit life is portrayed. The novel also discusses the classification issue of Mala-Madigas.

Plays

According to the research scholars, Korada Ramachandra Sastri's *Manjari Madhikariam* (1860) is considered as the first Telugu play. In his research on *Harijan Abhyudaya –Telugu Natakam* (1994: The Progress of Harijans and Telugu Play), V. Potanna discusses the issues of Madigas as portrayed in the plays. In his research, Potanna argues that the Mala-Madigas are Harijans. A perception is built up among Malas that only Madigas are Harijans not Malas. Potanna clarifies that several people address both Malas and Madigas as Harijans (1994:54). A few playwrights have given Madigas a unique place in their plays.

Boyi Bheemanna's *Raagavaashistam* (1959), the legendary-social play, delineates the love story of Arundhati and Vashista. It is said to be the first Telugu Dalit play. Vashistha Maharshi, a Brahmin, hesitates to marry

Arundhati when he comes to know her caste. At last, he realizes her committed devotion and nobility, and marries her. K. Chiranjeevi's *Neeli Deepaalu* (The Blue Lamps), a social play, depicts the atrocities of a landlord against a Madiga woman and her community for rebelling against his son who forces her into sex. *Parama Padam* (The Journey to Heaven), a social play, written by K.S.T Sai also reflects the same theme. Kolakaluri Enoch's play, *Munivahanudu*, portrays the story of Thiruppan who makes a successful attempt to enter the Sriranganatha temple. The story focuses on the life of Madigas. God would not object to entry and worship by a Madiga devotee, but the objection is raised by the priest. Kolakaluri Enoch, in another play, *Nirbhaya* (The Fearless), depicts the caste-based humiliation meted out to a Madiga student by his fellow students in the college. In another play, *Thyagi* (The Bestower), Kolakaluri Enoch greatly portrays the Madiga-Brahmin happy couple, but the conflict arises when they come to know their respective castes. This drama depicts that caste is insignificant when the coexistence of the people continues on their mutual understanding. *Ratnagarbhalo Nithya Daridrudu* (A Pauper on the Rich Land), a play written by M. Kanna Babu, portrays a Madiga who lives on his caste-based occupation. In *Harijanoddaranam* (Upliftment of Harijans), a play written by Maganti Paarthasarathi describes the love marriages of the Madiga-Brahmana varnas but the caste norms breed social conflicts. He suggests how to overcome such a sensitive problem. Patibandla Ananda Rao's play, *Nishiddaksharam* (The Banned Letter) describes how Madigas were denied education for generations in society. Thus, several plays have been produced portraying the Madiga life in different perspectives.

Several writers have written with the themes of untouchability, love, inter-caste marriages, disunity among Mala-Madigas and their social, cultural and economic conditions. For Madigas, traditional occupation gives them neither recognition nor economic sustenance. The plays written by Dalits provide different perspectives on the life of Madigas.

Conclusion

Madiga life is portrayed in different genres of Telugu literature. It is written in different perspectives and discussed in multiple dimensions. It is considered as an integral part of Dalit literature. In ancient Telugu literature, Dalits in general and Madigas in particular were described as untouchables. With the emergence of Dalit literature the concept of untouchability undergoes a lot of change that Madigas have secured their own cultural identity among all other untouchables. After fifty years of independence, Madigas began to be educated and they have started writing literature out of their own lived experiences. They have produced a lot of literature in different genres. Basically, Madiga literature reflects the culture of Madigas, it does not have a particular platform to share its way of life with mainstream literature. Even the media is not interested in spreading the spirit of Madiga culture around the world. Despite this fact, Madiga writers have started producing their literature and established a literary platform to share their experiences with other societies.

NOTES

1. *Andhra Mahabharatam*, 1-6.
2. It is a Sanskrit word that means precept, rules, manual, compendium, book or treatise in a general sense.

Subverting the Negative Images

Indian literary history has failed to adequately record the life of women lying unrecognized at the bottom of the society. Among those neglected are the Madiga sub-castes whose life is yet to be touched upon in the Telugu literary domain. The caste-based society in India has never recognized the productive castes whose contribution to the national income is tremendous. There exist about sixty-two Madiga sub-castes within the Dalit community across the two Telugu states of Telangana and Andhra Pradesh. The miseries of these sub-caste people are not textualized adequately. The caste pyramid, which has its strong roots in the Varna system, created a vertical order even among the lower castes. In this socially sub-categorized hierarchy, a dominant sub-caste of the same community looks down upon the other. Madiga is one of the principal sub-castes. It looks down upon its dependent castes like Dakkali, Chindu and Baindla within the community. Ironically Madigas are also looked down upon by Malas. The hierarchical order within the Dalit community gives a scope for superiority and inferiority complex, which is a replica of Varna order. However, all sub-castes of the Dalit community are discriminated against by the caste Hindus in Indian society.

During the Nizam regime in the Hyderabad Presidency in the pre-Independence time, all the lower castes including Dalits served the Nizam village official machinery such as

Police Patel and Malis Patel who used to take care of the law and order, and land revenue dealings respectively. Madigas were assigned to carry the post from one village to another village including the police stations. As a rule, they had to carry a faggot of fuel wood along with the post to hand over it to the addressee. They would get nothing in return but shoe-blows as a reward. A man or a woman from each family of the lower communities was compelled to render bonded labour. Dalits being landless poor made a major contribution to the village development. The Dominant upper castes are well aware of this fact. Dalits being the productive castes could bring the land under cultivation. Every caste Hindu knows the agrarian capabilities of Dalits.

In recognition to the collective labour, the *Nizam Sarkar*[1] gave a grant of gifted waste lands to them for cultivation, which were known as *Maannyem*[2] lands. These lands remained in the joint possession of the Madigas and other dependent castes like Dakkalis and Chindus at many places of Telangana state. Since Dakkalis and Chindus were dependent castes, they had no idea of agriculture. The 'caste tradition' confined them to singing and narrating the legends of the Madiga life and culture. Within the same colony, Madiga families are classified based on their ancestral lineage or *gotras*. Each Madiga lineage has several families. Each lineage group is again represented by the Madiga chief. *Maanyem* land is cultivated in turn by the respective families. The Madiga cultivator is supposed to offer 'Mannyem' to Dakkalis in lieu of their segment given to the former for cultivation.

In this discussion, two stories are taken from a Telugu anthology titled *Nalla Regadi Sallu* (Furrows of the Black

Soil). The title of this anthology is symbolic, in the sense that the life of the marginalized is linked to the agricultural land. Majority of the marginalized sections depend on their physical labour. No furrows are possible on farm lands without their toil. Jupaka Subhadra's "Maannyem" (The Gifted Land) and Gogu Shyamala's "Tataki", represent two different sub-castes. They deal with the question of land rights. In fact, one of the major issues is connected with the lives of the vulnerable. "Maannyem" portrays the rights of Dakkalis to claim 'Maanyem' and also their relationship with the Madigas while "Thataki" delineates how an attempt is made to seize the land back three generations ago, which was granted to the Madiga family under the land ceiling act.

The issue revolves around the land rights. It also discusses the relationship of Madigas with the dominant upper castes in rural Telangana. The two stories also portray how social relationships are maintained among the lower castes themselves and also with the upper castes. Jupaka Subhadra and Gogu Shyamala being insiders, write the stories of the Madiga life and culture in Telugu with full Madiga consciousness. They are part of the venerable village life. Characters deployed in their stories are not fictitious. They are real characters. Their stories are replete with real incidents. The characters pour out their lived experiences. Their portrayal is natural and it is wrought in the jargon of the illiterate Madiga sub-castes of the Telangana State.

Dakkali is a dependent caste of Madigas. Livelihood of the Dakkali community is precarious and owns no fixed settlements in any particular village. They are artists by profession. They keep on drifting from village to village throughout the year. Dakkalis live in makeshift shacks erected under trees on the fringes of the Madiga colonies. They tend to repeat their traditional claim that they are born from the ribs of Madigas and thus they declare themselves as their slaves. They also lay a claim for entitlement to food and 'mannyem' from the Madiga families in lieu of the land given to them (Madigas) for cultivation. They beg for food only from the Madiga families. "They share with the platter but not with the bed".

Rayakka, the protagonist in "Mannyem" is affectionately addressed by Madigas at least in her presence. In the beginning of the story, we notice her stepping into the village called Damaranchalapally in Warangal district of Telangana State where she decides to stay for fifteen days in order to claim her 'mannyem'. Though Madigas look down upon them in terms of hierarchy, they maintain cordial relations with their dependent castes. Muganna, a Madiga, affectionately enquires about Rayakka's journey and the well-being of the members of her family. He forges sisterly relations with Dakkali Rayakka. Jupaka Subhadra addresses Rayakka as Rajakka in her story. Though Madigas and Dakkalis do not exist together, they address affectionately one another.

A man belonging to the Mala caste is fascinated by the serpentine beauty of Rayakka. He breaks the caste rule of endogamy and steps into her life. He is a layman to the Dakkali profession. Rayakka tells stories with the help of other Dakkalis and narrates *Jambapuranam* glorifying the Madiga culture. She knows how to ward off evil by tying amulets to the sick. According to caste accord, Dakkalis are entitled to get food twice a day from the Madiga families. In fact, they act as spokespersons for Madigas and their culture.

Rayakka's father shares a half of forty villages with her as an offer of the bride-price. She is capable of arbitrating disputes between Madigas and Dakkalis.

Once, Rayakka complains to the Madiga chief about the denial of her legitimate share of 'mannyem' from Muthanna. He is supposed to offer it in lieu of her mannyem land. On Rayakka's complaint, the Madiga chief looks into the issue. In his enquiry, he comes to know the simple reason that Muttanna is also not allowed by his brother, Maisanna to cultivate the land throughout the year. So he is unable to give a share of paddy to Rayakka. Maisanna's response is that his brother did not give him money after selling some babul trees which are part of the maanyem land. Muttanna admits that due to some financial problems, he spends money for his own purpose. Rayakka, who is well aware of the complexity of the problem, sets a condition to both the Madiga brothers in a way that she should be given her legitimate share of grain or pay 'fine' in case of failure.

'Thataki' is one such short story that portrays how the landlords like Tirumala Rao; the Karnam Dora of the village attempt to seize the land back from Basaiah, the actual beneficiary. Basaiah's grandfather, Eeraiah, a farm labourer, was gifted the land by Venkat Rao, the grandfather of Tirumal Rao during the 'Bhoodan Movement'. Venkat Rao thinks that his farm labourer would never be able to cultivate it and at any time the land will be taken back from him. He wants to earn the name as a champion for the cause of the landless poor. But his plans are upset with the Government bringing his land under the ceiling act. Venkat Rao's heirs continue to seize the land from Basaiah.

Balamma, the daughter of Basaiah, is a girl of twelve. She is shrewd, courageous and heroic in her capabilities. She takes care of her ground-nut field in the absence of her father. Once her father admiringly remarks, "My father is reborn as Balamma" (Shyamala 34). Balamma, in her teens, is work-minded and punctual in her duties. She is unmatched in her work to any boy of her age. Yellaiah and Narsaiah are addressed affectionately as 'Yelladu' and 'Narsadu' by the elders and peers. Upper castes address the lower castes with derogatory suffixes which would debase and humiliate the Dalit culture. For instance, Thirumala Rao Dora addresses Basaiah as Bashega or Bashya in a twisted language to mean that the man is untouchable who does not deserve the original name or any refined or dignified name. The lower castes are invariably bound to address the dominant upper castes, Doras or Patels with utmost respect.

In her routine, Balamma wets her ground-nut field at the dawn thinking that others might deprive her of a legitimate share of water. In her innocence, she asserts her rights for equal share of water for her field. Her demand for a full share of water for her field enrages Tirumal Dora who calls her Thataka[3] or Thataki to give a sense of 'mischief'. Generally a mischievous person is termed Tataki. In the *Ramayana*, Tataki is projected as a demon. Gogu Shyamala subverts this negative image and deploys Thataki in her story as a heroine. She identifies Balamma with Thataki. Deconstructing the Hindu culture and the dominant attitude over the marginalized sections, she attempts to reconstruct the Madiga culture with a positive image of characters. Shyamala deliberately says 'yes'.

Balamma is Thataki in the positive terms of her acumen, intelligence and bravery. Her heroism is evident when she kicks on the private parts of Dora who in turn slaps on her cheek and even makes a vain bid to rape her.

Tirumala Dora plans to eliminate Balamma's father in order to deprive him of his land rights. Dora should have called Basaiah and her daughter to the public gathering if he intends to settle the dispute in an amicable way. But, in his arrogance, he takes law into his hands by dragging Balamma into the jawar fields when she is seen working alone. She undergoes a painful experience.

In "Mannyem" Rayakka complains to the Madiga chief when Muttaiah denies her legitimate share of paddy. But Muttaiah never tries to commit any atrocity against Rayakka like Tirumal Dora. However, the problem is settled amicably. These incidents testify to the fact that the relations between lower caste groups are cordial and democratic in approach while the relations between lower castes and upper castes are ever conflicting due to caste oppression and religious prejudice.

When Tirumal Dora holds her arm, she is surprised because upper caste people generally don't touch the untouchables. She understands that he is Tirumal Dora, a neighbour of her field. Grappling with him, she yells for help. She pleads with him to let her go. He arrogantly calls her a 'base born'. He further abuses her saying, "Are you a small child?" What is it that you have lost here and engaged in watering the field like a man? Do Malas and Madigas not have brains to keep their female children at home? For Tirumala Dora, the issue of sharing water for his field is just a pretext. Actually he is premeditated to seize the land back by threatening the Basaiah family. Even he thinks to the extent of eliminating Basaiah at any moment. He realizes that his evil deed would easily come out and he would get into trouble. He shifts his plan from elimination of Basaiah to commitment of atrocity against his daughter.

Rayakka never indulges in violence though she is denied her share of 'mannyem'. Madiga Pochavva refuses to offer food to Rayakka. But her refusal does not harm Rayakka at all. In the same way, the response of the two brothers given to Rayakka is not atrocious. She asserts her legitimate rights and fights with Madigas within the democratic framework. Rayakka's complaint to the Madiga chief would mean that she wants justice subject to caste accord. But the same attitude is not noticed in Tirumala Dora who breaks the natural principle of justice in solving his problem because he belongs to the dominant community. His decision is arbitrary and harmful, which results in the atrocity against the innocent girl.

Conclusion

The two stories are the best examples of how the marginalized people struggle for their survival that creates conflict with the upper castes. "Mannyem" is a powerful Madiga-Dakkali story that highlights power structure and cultural variations within the same community. Caste hierarchy defines this power structure in different terms. The 'Madiga Caste Accord' is still in practice in Telangana villages. This practice strengthens the endogamous community life on one hand and it is broken to some extent with inter sub-caste-marriages like Mala man marrying a Dakkali woman. In 'Thataki,' the Hindu dominant culture represented by Tirumal Rao is subverted and the culture of productive castes represented by the Balamma family is valorized and strengthened. The argument is built in favour of the land rights. Cultivation of land is a sole means of the majority Dalits for their life sustenance. Dismantling of sub-caste structures within the communities would pave the way for collective liberation from the upper caste oppression.

"Mannyem" shown in double quote indicates the title of the story while 'Mannyem' shown in a single quote means an agricultural land belonging to the Dakkali caste (a nomadic caste dependent on Madigas) gifted to the Madigas for cultivation in lieu of which the latter have to offer the former mannheim, which also means a fixed quantity of paddy grain.

NOTES

1. Nizam was the title of the native sovereigns of Hyderabad State, India, since 1719. They belonged to the Asaf Jahi dynasty. The dynasty was founded by Mir Qamar-ud-Din Siddiqi, a viceroy of the Deccan under the Mughal emperors from 1713 to 1721. Seven Nizams ruled Hyderabad for two centuries until Indian independence in 1947.
2. The gifted land was given to Dalits by the Nizam government and which also means a fixed quantity of paddy to be offered to Dakkali as per tradition.
3. Thataka was a Yaksha princess and daughter and only child of the Yaksha king Suketu, she was a beautiful princess that was wooed by and married Sunda, a Rakshas. She bore Sunda two sons, Subahu and Maricha. Taraka would harass and attack rishis performing yajnas in the forest. They were ultimately slain by Rama and Lakshmana on behest of their teacher, maharishi Vishwamitra. But the story writer glorified the demon as a hero and made a heroic character in the story.

Drumming and Tanning as Cultural Identity

It is said that the Dravidians were the rulers of ancient India. They were known as *Asurarajas* (the demon kings) or *Asura Ghana*. They were also called Dasyas. They belonged to the ancient Naga decency. They were victims of the Aryan invasions. They settled at many places in various denominations. They were politically, economically, socially and morally oppressed. These oppressed Mala-Madiga social groups are called Dalits. Malas in Telugu states are considered equivalent to Mahars in Maharashtra while Madigas in Telugu states are equivalent to Chamars in northern states of India. Chamars are highly concentrated in the north while Mahars are more in number in Maharashtra. It is needless to say that Malas and Madigas are of the same offspring.

Madigas constitute more than 75 lakh in United Andhra. But in Andhra Pradesh, Madiga population is much less while in Rayalaseema region it is little more. The present Telangana State has a lot of Madiga population compared to Malas. Mahbubnagar, Gadwal, Nagarkarnool, Narayanapet districts which constitute high Madiga population, stand first in place among other districts of Telangana State while East Godavari and Nalgonda districts stand second and third respectively in divided Andhra Pradesh. 'Mala' is an advanced social group in all spheres of life when compared to any other sub-caste group within the Dalit community. In terms of population, Malas are just more than a half of the Madiga population. Though Madigas almost double the Mala population, Malas have gained upper hand in every field. The book, *Reservation Madigala Emi Chesisindi?*(What Reservations have done to the Madigas?), foregrounds the socio-economic and political circumstances of the Madiga community. Why have the Madigas lagged behind? Did reservations not support them? Which social group has been enjoying the constitutional benefits for the last more than fifty years? This situation prompts every sensible person to ask whether there is a flaw in the implementation of the reservation or exploitation is unleashed in the guise of the Dalit community. It is an open secret that the dominant groups indulge in exploitation of reservation benefits in any caste society.

Basically, Madigas are tanners by profession. Most of the families depended upon the tanning work in earlier times. They would skin the animals which were lying dead in front of the houses of the upper castes. They would convert the raw hides of the cattle into leather through a tanning process which would take about a month to obtain usable leather. It can be used for agricultural needs and in shoemaking as well. This work provided them with some livelihood to some extent in the past. Though there is a change in their caste-based occupation, some Madiga families still continue to depend upon leather work in rural India. Most of the Madiga families are still working as farm hands with the upper caste landlords. The Madiga families are seen working even with the economically advanced groups of their own community people and also with the Backward Castes as well. The fact is that in urban areas, economically weaker sections are also working as domestic hands in the houses of their fellow

Backward Castes. There are instances of the upper caste poor who are also doing domestic work in the houses of the wealthy social groups of the lower order. This is the present scenario of various social categories. It is a very rare case to think that Brahmin women would work with Dalit families. In urban milieu caste identities do not seem to be as strong as in the rural milieu. Migrant workers and settlers with different social background are involved in the works not related to their caste. For them, labour is a common identity. However, they are still fond of retaining their caste traditions and expose them during festivals and other celebrations.

Besides tanning, Madigas are involved in making drums with the semi-tanned hide of a young buffalo. They make drums themselves with the available material. Only a few Madiga individuals from Madiga families are skilled in making and drumming. It is a sleek, flat-faced drum which is made of the skin of buffaloes, cows or goats. It catches the attention of a listener instantly. An instrument with a significant connotation socially, culturally and politically, it is one of India's oldest types of drums. It is called in varied names like *Dappu* or *Thappeta* in Telugu states, *Thappu* or *Parai* in Tamil Nadu and *Daff* in Maharashtra etc.

Madiga drummers go in bands for drum-beating for upper caste people on auspicious occasions. Drum-beating is allowed along with band music played by the individuals of the barber community. Madiga drum-beater gets less wages than that of a band musician. This variation may be because of caste status and quality of the music instruments used by the drummers. A drum of the Madiga is less rated than that of the barber's musical instrument. Most of the illiterate Madiga youths tended to give up their caste-based drumming and pursued other lucrative professions for better earning and dignified living in urban areas.

Katika or butcher community is considered as a lower caste. He lives on selling beef. *Chekka Thuraka* or a Muslim of the lower community owns the tanning factories and purchases raw hides of cattle from Madigas. This practice has disappeared in most of the villages.

A few individuals of the Madiga families go for peeling off *tangedu*[1] by beating the wood with a club. After breaking the peel, it is dried in the sun. These shrubs are usually grown on hillocks. Afterwards, they sell the dried peels to the Muslim tanners who purchase in bulk for use in tanning process. Some Madigas work in Muslim factories too. Several Madiga children have not been blessed with education. Only a few Madigas with higher education entered the government positions.

There is also other side of Madigas. Some Madiga individuals are higher ups too, who cannot be reached out by the common folk of their community. This fact cannot be denied. The poor Madigas get nothing from the flourished Madigas who do not seem to have a concern for a fellow Madiga. Some Dalit elitist individuals have become a class which befriends the equivalent classes of the other communities not with the individual of their own community. Creamy layer part is the other side of Madiga community. It is as true as in any other community. This would not contribute to the equal development of the Dalit community nor would it be helpful in the achievement of unity and integrity among the individuals of a community.

Malas have nothing to do with the tanning work from any point of time. They have not been associated with skinning dead animals and tanning their hides. *Bagari* is one of the sub-castes of Mala community in the Telugu states. In fact, *Bagaris* are grave-diggers. It is not that the majority of Malas do this work. They are associated with the occupation of grave-digging for the castes above theirs in the social ladder. They also help the *Boyas* in cremating the dead. But, they do not perform the same for Madigas.

Malas do not make any conventional marital alliances with Madigas. There may be sporadic love marriages that might have exceptionally taken place between the two sub-castes. There is a devotional divide as both the groups worship the village deities at separate places in the village. Even today, at several places of the Telugu states, Malas do not allow Madigas to go into their houses nor do they allow them to touch their cooking utensils. In terms of caste hierarchy, Malas stand high above all other lower castes within the Dalit community. Several upper caste people do not know this fact. Economically advanced groups among Madigas also cannot escape from caste discrimination. Despite these disparities among Dalits, they are equally victims of caste prejudice and religious discrimination perpetrated by the upper castes.

When coastal Andhra was under the British regime, Malas were part of the development activities carried out by the British officials. Christian missionaries established schools and hospitals at several places of the erstwhile Andhra region. Most of the Malas were appointed as teachers. The Mala women joined the Primary Health centres as nurses and doctors. Thus, they got a lot of employment opportunities. They were associated with welfare activities too. They were very interested in health and education. Lutherans and Baptists carried out developmental activities across Coastal Andhra.

Lutherans were rich people. They established missionaries across the world. They also founded educational institutions, hospitals and churches in Andhra region too. Lutherans helped Malas in their advancement because of close relations between them. Almost all Mala converts were Lutherans. Malas occupied several positions as teachers, doctors, nurses and church pastors across Andhra region. Through Christian religion, they were able to easily forge international relations and had an opportunity to study all kinds of developmental activities in foreign countries.

Their association with foreign people helped them to enrich a sense of self-respect and self-confidence while Madigas were not blessed with such opportunities at any point of time. Baptists are those who rebelled against the Lutherans and came out. They were termed as revolutionaries among the Christians. Baptists were disassociated with the tyrannical Catholics and they declared themselves as independent of Lutherans and Catholics as well. In that they were not exposed much to education. Madigas who were associated with the Baptists could not flourish like Malas. Since the Baptists were economically poor even in foreign countries, they could not do anything to the Madiga Christians in Andhra region. There was also a debate on social relations between Malas and Madigas given the above conditions.

In fact, Malas are reluctant to forge any alliance with Madigas from any point of view as they fear that they would also go down to the level of the Madiga existence. Malas have never done the so-called contemptuous skinning or tanning or shoemaking. They were never involved in drum-beating either. Thus, several Andhra Malas got an opportunity for education which increasingly enriched their social consciousness as well. This enabled them to grab disproportionate reservation benefits. For instance, in the United Andhra, 39 constituencies were reserved for Scheduled Castes. On the basis of population, Madigas should have been allotted 24, but only 12 constituencies were given to them. In the same way, they were given only two out of six parliamentary seats. Madigas alleged that most of the seats were grabbed by Malas alone.

Madigas are dismayed by the unwanted developments in contemporary times. Surprisingly, all the seats in Municipal elections were bagged by Malas per se. At last, a Mayor post too went in their favour. In this backdrop, there was a fair demand by Madigas for distribution of seats in the parliament in proportion to the population. Against the spirit of the constitution, Malas have grabbed more chances than they deserve. Only Mala individuals were appointed as chairpersons and directors of (United) Andhra Pradesh Study Circle, Andhra Pradesh Social Welfare Department and Andhra Pradesh Scheduled Castes Corporation etc. Madigas are of the view that Government schemes being intended to benefit the downtrodden among Scheduled Castes are going in favour of Malas only. Thus they are unilaterally enjoying the constitutional benefits. The fact is that majority IAS and IPS officers in secretariats of the Telugu states and professors in the universities absolutely belong to the Mala community.

As alleged by Madigas, Malas are grabbing the legitimate chances from Madigas and other sub-castes in every sphere. This is one side of the coin. The other side of the coin is 'creamy layer' which is an existing reality among both Malas and Madigas within the community. These two main castes ignore 57 sub-castes and dependent castes and a class flourishes at the cost of these dependent castes lying at the bottom. 'Advanced section' or the 'creamy layer' from both the castes tends to emulate upper caste Hindu culture and support the ruling class in all possible ways in order to curry favour with them. This divisive strategy will hinder the progress of a fellow Dalit. The unemployed majority of marginalized communities criticize the dominant upper castes in power ignoring the fact that their fellow Dalit Bhavujan leaders are in support of the upper castes. The concept of equal development of all sub-castes would continue to be a mirage.

It is needless to say that the higher positions are grabbed by the children of the advanced classes within the Dalit community which predominantly constitute Mala and Madiga groups. Poor children from the same community cannot compete with those of the rich due to improper education, poverty, poor guidance and zero social awareness. Given this situation, those who are in high position grow higher while the low position becomes lower. This creates socio-economic imbalances among the downtrodden people. Keeping in view social justice, rulers need to relax the educational qualifications of the target candidates for employment opportunities.

A *gurukula* system of education trains the select few from among the marginalized communities. It might be a good scheme but it would ultimately create a 'creamy layer' among the oppressed in the long run. The educated Dalit babus' will be at the helm of affairs to control the disadvantaged majority within the Dalit community per se.. The majority children of the oppressed community would become a 'servant class' for the so called meritorious few educated in convent and *Gurukula* schools. This system of education breeds the elitist group in the name of merit which is created at the cost of the majority underprivileged children who are confined to government schools deprived of basic facilitates.

It is reported that in many cases, upper castes are also exploiting the reservation benefits by in the act of impersonation. For upper castes, obtaining reservation certificates through manipulation from the Mandal level officials is an easy task in villages. All the lower-castes, cutting across the sub-caste distinctions, can collectively fight against the mischief of impersonation by the upper castes. For want of unity among Dalits, which may be a distant dream due to disparities, such a collective task is never planned. Disunity among these lower castes by reason of sub-caste gradation and economic disparities, mobilization of the Dalit forces is becoming a mirage.

When the advanced section indulges in (mis)appropriation of the reservation benefits, the backward section within the community would do nothing. The trend appears not only with the Scheduled Castes and Tribes but among the 'backward classes too'. It is because the 'demon of creamy layer' can exist in any reservation community. In this backdrop, a demand for classification of the existing pattern of reservation into ABCD groups has come to the fore. This would serve as "a squint eye in place of the blind one". Given the inappropriate distribution of the reservation benefits, the classification demand would create a sort of hope for democratic distribution and constitutional fairness in the enjoyment of the equal rights and opportunities meant for the disadvantaged groups.

In those days, Dr. B.R Ambedkar fought for social justice and equality for the cause of his community. He would have put forth a demand for the ABCD categorization for equal constitutional benefits with the same social consciousness if he were alive today. Will it not be injustice on the part of the advanced Dalit section to continue to enjoy reservation benefits unilaterally? One can recollect Dr. Ambedkar's words, "I never thought that the advanced Dalit groups, neglecting the lower order within the community, would play a clerical role with the upper castes."

Demand for classification of reservation benefits should also include keeping 'creamy layer' off the reservation frame to enable the distribution of its fruits to the lowest of the low within the Dalit community per se for true social and economic justice. Several Mala brethren have misunderstood this demand as dividing the Dalits. The demand for classification of reservation benefits, to some extent, would address the core part of the problem. However, it cannot eliminate the basic socio-economic imbalances, but it might minimize the disparities among the sub-castes and dependent castes as well.

The Madiga sub-caste group has become more conscious and realized that only one dominant sub-caste group has been enjoying the reservation benefits from its inception. Looking at the employment statistics, Madiga group is still lagging behind in reaching out to its legitimate share. Madigas have woken up late to the constitutional safeguards. From this backdrop, "*Madiga Hakkula Dandora Movement*" (A Dandora Movement for Madiga Rights) emerged. This movement emphasized the classification of reservation into ABCD groups in proportion to the population of each sub-caste within the community. It exerted political pressure on various political parties to constitute a Commission to look into the issue. A One-man Commission with Justice Ramachandra Raju was set up. After thorough study, the Commission submitted its report to the Government. But the Commission's findings/ recommendations were not properly implemented by the successive governments due to legal impediments created by the rival group.

Conclusion

Socio-economic issues are linked to the sub-caste groups of Malas and Madigas. Though both the groups have almost a similar socio-cultural life, sub-caste has created a feeling of gradational superiority by Malas. All the sub-caste groups are branded as untouchable castes including Malas and Madigas. The sub-caste hierarchy, which is duplicated from the Varna system, all the sub-caste groups being scattered all over the state will hardly come together for coexistence. A few inter-caste marriages among them would be an exception, which mostly happen between advanced groups for economic reasons. Social inequality, economic disparities between these groups further cause a divide. This has created socio-economic and political imbalances. In this backdrop, *the Madigu Hakkula Dandora Movement* emerged seeking constitutional protection and legitimate reservation benefits by way of classification for equal rights and social justice. This debate raked up in order to highlight how a dominant section within the same community has grabbed the constitutional benefits from the fellow groups which are still lagging behind in all spheres of human life.

NOTE

1. A kind of bushy plant with thick peel. A Cassia shrub grown on hillocks.

Ethnic Culture and Tradition: A Comparative Reading of Igbo and Madiga

It is a known fact that several Nations were under European colonial rule for centuries. The native cultures of the colonial counties were subordinated, marginalized and even marred beyond trace. Blatant denial of freedom to the native people took place. They were deprived of their own country's riches. Their tongue was gagged and their voice was suppressed. It was strange but a painful experience that left them disappointed and helpless. The experience of colonization all over the world is almost the same. Incidentally, African countries and India were under Western colonial governance. They were utterly helpless in their claim over their native culture and identity. It is a historical fact that every community within the nation has its own culture and tradition that characterizes its way of life, and its people are proud of their cultural regimes and traditional belief systems.

The western cultural onslaught totally disturbed the peaceful coexistence of the African Igbo people. The entire colonial system was responsible for disintegration among the Africans. In ancient India, there were different tribes that existed in units or groups with cultural autonomy. "They were the indigenous people of the region descended from Neolithic settlers who have been incorporated into the caste system as general manual labourers for agriculture and leather working" (Web 1). They enriched the Harappa civilization. Horizontal living was a manifestation of socio-cultural equality among various tribes. Social fabric of the tribal groups was disturbed with the advent of the Aryans into India. The Varna system which originated from Aryanic life became a curse for the Indian Dalits because they (Black Untouchables) were/have been socially and culturally victimized more by the Hindu caste system than by the British Colonial Rule. The marginalized groups in general and Dalits in particular had a horrendous experience which continues down to the present of course with less intensity but in different forms.

Dalit community has several sub-castes with multiple gradations within and serves as a replica of Varna system. One such significant sub-caste is Madiga that constitutes the highest population among other fifty-eight sub-castes in the State alone. The Madiga community is spread across the northern and southern states of India in different nomenclatures. Madiga is a significant sub-caste with an assertion for a dignified social life and social identity. Madigas draw their caste myth called 'Jambapurana' that delineates the genesis of the Madiga caste and cultural past. Their contribution to society through their art and other essential services is significant. In fact, Madigas are not tribes like Igbos in Nigeria. They are socially and culturally excluded people. Though they were the sons of the Indian soil, they were pushed to the fringes of the village settlements. Thus they were excluded from the mainstream social life which amounted to discrimination and oppression. In fact, they were enslaved by the Aryans who invaded India and disturbed their peaceful co-existence.

History speaks of India and Africa as one land mass until it was separated by the ocean. "The Dalits were the original inhabitants of India and resemble the African in physical features" (Rajasekhar 43). In the light of this fact, some scholars like V.T. Rajasekhar termed the natives of the country as India's black untouchables. The historical fact is that the conquered natives of India, who were compelled to serve the Aryan order, were thrown on the village peripheries, while others who refused to serve the Aryans fled to the forests and hills only to become tribes with no fixed settlements. A study of their historical evolution shows that the Scheduled Castes and Tribes had a common ancestral lineage before the advent of the Aryans. The life of the rural Madigas constitutes an integral part of the Dalit community in both the Telugu states.

Apart from the historical life in India, *Jambapurana* serves as a cultural Bible for Madigas. It gives a good speculation on the origin of the Madiga community. "When a cow of plenty dies on the top of the mountain called *Sanjeevani,* there is none to bring down its carcass. Then the gods address 'Jambavamuni as Mahadigira'. With the passage of time Maha-Adiga became Madiga, which would mean the man descending from above". Madigas are said to be the offspring of Jambavamuni. On the origin of Madigas, *Jambapurana* narrates as to how all the gods desired to eat dead cow of plenty and decided not to waste any part of it. On their request, Jambavamuni, with his nails, chops the flesh into pieces. He directs his son, Chennaiah, to cook it. While cooking, the boy puts back into the pot a soiled piece of flesh from the floor. His act enrages the gods and consequently they curse the boy that all his heirs would live on dead carrion and become untouchables who would be confined only to the fringes of the actual villages.

Igbo and Madiga are two different terms in social and cultural context. The Igbo are the people in eastern Nigerian while the Madigas are so-called social untouchables who are widely spread across India with different names. 'Igbo' is a clan that characterizes the pluralistic tribal life of the African natives. Chamarras in the North, Mangs in Maharashtra, Madigas in Karnataka and Chakkiliyan in Tamil Nadu are one and the same in their cultural and social life in India. They are traditionally associated with skinning dead animals in order to produce leather through a tanning process. This work created a livelihood for them. "Like all castes in India, today they generally believe in prestigious origins. One such theory speculates that Madiga is derived from Sanskrit word Maha-Adiga which can be loosely translated as "great and olders" (Web 2).

Both Igbos and Madigas can be juxtaposed in terms of cultural life and traditional ways. Of course, Madigas are branded as untouchables while the Igbo are not untouchables in their native land. They ruled their land themselves unlike in India where Madigas and other Dalits are still living as the subjects not the rulers. Indian tribes who have nomadic experience are not untouchables like Madigas. Both the groups are excluded from the Indian mainstream life for some historical reason or the other. Their life has roots in the primeval co-existence of the aboriginals. Madigas and tribes had a common lineage in ancient times but their social life became unique due to the Indian caste system. Both India and Africa underwent colonial experience.

Christian missionaries actively operated in both the countries. Conversion activities went on in full swing in the established colonies and many educational institutions came up for the colonized. The British regime strongly impacted the Coastal Andhra area of the Madras Presidency while the Hyderabad State, which was under the Nizam's rule, was not blessed with colonial (English) education. Colonial conditions were similar in both the countries.

Chinua Achebe's *Things Fall Apart* (1958) is a fine delineation of the ancestral customs and traditions of the Igbo people in Eastern Nigeria of the 1890s. The novel seeks to discover the cultural ethos of the Igbo society. The way of worshipping *Allah* or *Ali,* the Earth goddess, by the Igbo is analogous to the worship of *Bhoolaxmi* performed by Madigas. Worship of the local goddesses by the lower castes provides a perfect similarity in terms of their traditional beliefs and customs. Local goddess who blesses the farming community with flourishing crops forges a kind of harmonious relationship between the lower castes. Similarly, the social customs in the Igbo community would reflect a kind of social harmony which was strengthened by their customs and culture. The social harmony of the village, Umuofia, is evoked vividly through Achebe's presentation of the customs and traditions extending from birth, through marriage to death, and of the educational, religious, and hierarchical systems' ' (Varalaxmi 58-59).

Achebe's Okonkwo, the protagonist in the novel, represents the pre-colonial Nigerian of inflexible customs, complex culture and traditional dignity. Apart from *Bhoolaxmi*, Madigas worship their caste deities like *Balamma, Mashamma, Pochamma, Yellamma* and

Poleramma who are different from Hindu gods like *Laxmi, Saraswathi, Parvati, Durga Mata and Kalika Devi*. These deities are worshipped during festivals and harvests. They firmly believe that the caste goddesses protect them from diseases like Cholera and Smallpox. "Rituals and ceremonies of the Madigas mirror the space that the women had in the spiritual world. Dalits had recognized the feminine dimension of the deity and it is evident in the fact that in most of the cases deity manifested Her (Him) -self in the form of feminine" (Web 4).

Madigas are hard-working people who have been cleansing the dirt of Hindus for centuries. Thus they are serving the Hindu Society. Igbo are also hard-working people and Okonkwo stands as one of the best examples. Owning barns filled with yams is an indication of prosperity and it manifests the merit of the Head of the family. The hard work they put in on their own farms yields them prosperity for a joyful life. The Madiga majorities do not own lands and so most of them either work as agricultural labourers or they are relegated to their caste based traditional occupations.

Apart from animal sacrifice to the village goddesses, other ritualistic performances take place in both the societies. Achebe does not hesitate to point out the flaws that are also part of the African / Igbo legacy. For instance, abandoning of the twins and the sick people in the Evil Forest was considered an abomination to the Earth, and the ritualized human sacrifices intended to appease the deities indicate 'cruelty of traditional customs'. Ikemefuna's brutal killing to appease the Oracle is a strong case in point. Such rituals can be understood as the dark side of the community. In the Madiga cultural world, such practices had/have no place in Madiga cultural life either in the past or in the present.

As per the marriage system, Madigas still practice endogamy. The endogamous consciousness is linked to the Madiga identity. To them, bigamy or polygamy would attract punishment as they are governed by the Hindu law. For Igbo, no punishment is awarded for such practices. They choose endogamy because they feel that "Exogamy creates a system of affiliations and communications larger than that of the autonomous village" (Carroll 15). In societal aspects of marriage, both the Igbos and the Madigas seem to have a similar traditional concept of protecting their community.

Religious context is central to the Igbos' three-tier belief. It is a veneration of *Chukwu*,[1] a supreme deity in traditional Igbo mythology. The belief of the Igbos is that *Chukwu* created the world. The Igbos worshipped their ancestors and they had the cult of personal god or *chi.* Chukwu is the god without a shrine or a priest. Sky is his abode and he is the god of creation and fertility like Brahma in Hindu mythology. "Igbo mythology seems to emphasize the principle of dualism as against monism or absolutism" (Reddy 25). '*Chi*'[2] is a generic word for god; it is a sort of personal god. It is a part of *Chukwu*. The Igbo personal spirit is akin to the Indian concept of Karma. *Chikwu* and *Chi* can also be taken on par with *atman* or *atma*[3] (soul) and *parmatma*[4] (universal soul) the Indian religious context. Hindus firmly believe that the individual *atma* would ultimately merge into *paramathma*, the supreme God. Every Hindu including Dalits has been indoctrinated with the *karma* theory for centuries. The majority of Madigas, who have not embraced other faiths, are still considered part of

Hindu religion. They still share the religious belief of the Hindus. So they have become firm believers of the *Karma* theory.

In the world of Madiga music, *Dappu* plays a significant role. It is also called *Tappeta* (drum) in some areas of the Telugu states. A round frame for *Dappu* is made either from wood or metal. Wood is preferably used for a lightweight. The frame is covered with a half-tanned hide of a buffalo calf. *Dappu* requires technical skills in its playing. "The drumbeat is so powerful that even people at a distance of two miles would be prompted into rhythmic steps. It will produce exactly the same beat the latest musical instrument Jazz drums give" (Web 2). Commenting on the Dalit-Bahujan contribution to society, Kancha Ilaiah' says: "Dalit-Bahujan[5] masses have enormous technological and engineering skills that are not divorced from their labour. One who lifts dead cattle also knows the science of skinning it. They themselves know how to process the skin and make chappals, shoes, or ropes. All these tasks involve physical labour."

Skinning dead cattle and tanning are done only by Madigas not by all Dalit-Bahujans. Skinning dead cattle is considered as an act of defilement. Traditional occupations such as skinning, tapping toddy, making pots and so on are demarcated on caste lines. Toddy tapping and pot-making are given a different status when compared to skinning animals; there is also a hierarchy in traditional professions as seen in different castes.

Every Madiga does not necessarily participate in the traditional occupation of drumming. Only interested youth participate in the art of drum-beat; because, only a few people know it. Several Madigas are farm labourers. In changing social circumstances, the affluent Madigas are associated with politics and other spheres of human life.

Migration of the Madiga youth takes place on a large scale due to unavailability of labour work in cities and towns. The traditional occupation of drum-beating by Madigas is almost given up for lack of interest to continue it. For Igbos, drum-beating is part of their tradition. Some interested Madiga youth skilled in drum beating choose it as a means of livelihood. Drum-beating generally takes place during marriages and festivals. Igbo people play drum-beat as per their custom not as part of their livelihood. In the Igbo community, *Kola* is broken and wine is offered to visiting guests. Guests customarily bring with them a goat-skin to sit on. Madigas also offer either toddy or arrack to the guests on their occasional visits.

Customary settlement of bride-price takes place in both the societies of Igbos and Madigas. 'Bride-price', a social practice still continues in some Telangana villages. Unlike dowry, "bride-price" is given to the bride a little before or during marriages. The rural marginalized societies still adopt a custom known as *kanyasulkam* (bride-price). The majority poor and illiterate rural Madigas still practice this custom. Only a few affluent lower castes tend to go with the upper castes and emulate the practice of dowry. On the whole, economically affluent sections indulge in such practices regardless of their social category. '*Oli*' is an equivalent term for '*kanyasulkam*' which is mostly used in the southern part of Telangana state. Practice of '*Oil'* is analogous to *Uri* that existed in the Igbo society too. *Uri* and *Oli* appear as two different nomenclatures for the same social purpose and practice.

Telugu is one of the Indian languages spoken by the people of all social categories in both the states of Telangana and Andhra Pradesh with a dialectal variation. The dialect of the Madigas is not different from that of other Dalit sub-castes and upper-caste Hindus as well within the village, but regionally the dialect varies among Madigas and other castes too. Occupation-based terms are also dialectically different among Madiga groups belonging to different regions of the Telugu states. Thus it is inferred that Madigas are a single community that speaks with different regional and local dialectical variations. It is true with the Igbo community too. "Cultural uniformity is an important dimension in the Igbo community. They are a single people speaking a number of related dialects with many social features in common" (Carroll, 13).

Despite cultural divergences between two different societies of Igbo and Madiga, some similarities are clearly discerned in their traditional life. However, social and cultural circumstances are certainly different in their juxtapositions. Comparison or contrast can be drawn between certain social customs of the two societies. Of course, Igbo society is not a segregated society like Dalits, but both the societies are linked to an agrarian pattern of life with exceptions of caste based 'untouchable' occupations.

NOTES

1. Chukwu is the supreme being of Igbo spirituality. In the Igbo pantheon, Chukwu is the source of all other Igbo deities and is responsible for assigning them their different tasks. The Igbo people believe that all things come from Chukwu, who brings the rain necessary for plants to grow and controls everything

on Earth and the spiritual world. They believe Chukwu to be an undefinable omnipotent and omnipresent supreme deity that encompasses everything in space and space itself.

2. The Igbo believe that an individual's fate and abilities for the coming life are assigned to the chi, and each individual is given a chi by the Creator (Chukwu) at the moment of conception.
3. Atman means 'eternal self'. The ***atman*** refers to the real self beyond ego or false self. It is often referred to as 'spirit' or 'soul' and indicates our true self or essence which underlies our existence.
4. Parmatma refers to the highest soul and God.
5. Kancha Ilaiah is Professor of Political Science at Osmania University, Hyderabad. He is a Dalit-Bahujan campaigner who has used this term in his writings. Bahujan literally means 'the many or majority: people (masses) who have been deprived of humanity for centuries in contrast to a handful who take their pleasure, call themselves superior and live at the cost of the masses'. The Bahujan are productive castes whose contribution to national economic development is immense. Since Bahujans include Dalits, it is rephrased as Dalit-Bahujans.

Valmiki's *Joothan* and Joshua's *Naakatha* as Narratives of Lived Experiences

The erstwhile untouchables of India known as Dalits today, who were thrown at the bottom of the caste pyramid, have been victims of consequent social discrimination and religious prejudice. The Indian social fabric systematically denied them freedom, education and the right to speak. They were made voiceless and in that they experienced oppressive social conditions. They have inherited the same even today. Though these were the issues of the past, their relics are strong and visible indifferent forms in the present. Despite superficial changes, Ekalavyas in Indian society are still grappling with learning amidst modern Dronacharyas. Though Indians lingered under the duress of colonial rule, at least a few people of the oppressed community must have had colonial education for their social betterment, thanks to Christian missionaries which spread education among the lower strata of society in British India.

In the past, mainstream Indian literature was monopolized by a class of writers belonging to hegemonic communities and literature was treated as being noble, produced by the so-called highly placed individuals. The characters created by them from the lower strata of society. Their writings were shown either as objects of pathos or victims of social suffering in exigency of a savior. In most of the works produced by the privileged class, protagonists are deployed from the upper stratum of society. In case of the protagonist hailing from the lower stratum in their sympathetic writings, characters are often made voiceless and incapable of responding to social humiliation. Transformation of the stigmatized social status of the ex-untouchables to a self-chosen identity as Dalit is a clear manifestation of social assertion. Dalits began to write poetry subverting the Hindu canon. Protest was an element deployed in their writing against the established social system. Dalit writers, who have been educated in the vernacular, have begun to use autobiography as an important genre or a literary weapon to narrate their lived experiences. Writing itself is made as an institutional space to enter the public sphere. Thus Dalit autobiography has become a potential means of social assertion.

In the present context of the Dalit-self, it is relevant to go into the testimonial literature of the natives of Latin America. Testimonial literature was produced on behalf of the indigenous victims. The emergence of testimonial literature is a manifestation of recording a vibrant protest against the prevalent situation in the country. Testimonial literature emerged as a back-lash against mainstream society. In the same way autobiographical writing emerged as a response to mainstream writing in India. Quoting Rigoberta Menchu, Coral A. Walker says: "A testimony can encompass more than just the story of one individual, but rather it is the story of a marginalized group. This is my testimony. I didn't learn it from a book and I didn't learn it alone. I'd like to stress that it's not only my life, it's also testimony of my people. ... The important thing is that what has happened to me has happened to many other people too.

My story is the story of all poor Guatemalans. My personal experience is the reality of a whole people" (1).

Menchu's views clarify as to how the prevalent social, political and economic circumstances of one's native soil compel the educated oppressed to produce testimonies as a counter narration against mainstream writing. Dalit autobiographies as counter narratives can be located within the domain of testimonial writing, of course; with a different social problem. "Literature is often used as a way to naturalize political ideology, and it is often produced by the members of the dominant classes in society who tend to represent and naturalize differences as it is from their social and cultural position" (Guelberger and Kearney np). Latin America suffered exploitation, political instability and elimination by colonization. The indigenous people were unable to represent themselves through literature as it was dominated by the elitist classes. Dalit autobiographical writing emerged as parallel narrative to the mainstream writing in India. It is more or less analogous to testimonial literature in Latin America. Testimonial literature is "an authentic literature told by a witness who is moved to narrate by the urgency of a situation (e.g. war, oppression, revolution etc.). In India, Dalit autobiographical literature is produced by a victim who is compelled to narrate his/her lived experiences in the wake of the chronic caste discrimination.

In India, Dalits have been the worst sufferers of the caste system which evolved a rigidly structured society. Caste oppression is the cause of urgency which moved Dalit writers to narrate their lived experiences in their autobiographies. It is an authentic document of a collective suffering represented by an individual. Given its basic tenets,

Dalit autobiography can be placed in the dominion of testimonial literature. Writing about 'self' has become· a strong voice of the voiceless representing the community. On the realist view of representation, Miguel Barnet contends that "testimonial literature seeks to establish identities between protagonist and collective, between researcher and protagonist ·and consequently, between reader, researcher, protagonist, and collective, between ·present subject and objective history, and between written and the living spoken language" (Colas 161). Dalit autobiography as a social document establishes identity between the protagonist and the collective as the writer himself/ herself is the protagonist.

In this chapter, two Dalit autobiographies have been chosen from different language cultures i.e. Hindi and Telugu for comparative reading - Omprakash Valmiki's *Joothan* (Scraps 1996) and Gurram Joshua's *Naa Katha* (1966: My Story). Both of them suffered caste humiliation in their respective social environments. Valmiki's Chura community with an ascribed social status outside the *chaturvarna* sets his life story in north India, just around the time when our constitution outlawed untouchability. *Joothan* was originally written in Hindi, which delineates the social consciousness of the first and second generation. The autobiography transforms the stigma of untouchability into Valmiki's Dalit identity.

Gurram Joshua, who was born of a couple from two different caste backgrounds, endured social ostracism and extreme poverty. His parentage was associated with Christianity. In that he was a Christian by religion. The caste Hindus who were dominant in his· native village, Vinukonda, treated him with contempt. Christians too alienated him as he was reading the Hindu scriptures. People of both the religions failed to understand Joshua's innate nature of religious harmony and the sense of universalism, instead they ostracized him. Social expulsion from society was a reward bestowed on him for his secular approach towards religion. Only the mosque came to his rescue in such a troubled situation.

Valmiki's *Joothan* is a flaming rhetoric that pervades his entire autobiography. It is highly inflated with interrogations on caste discrimination, poverty, religious prejudice and social alienation. It is a social document enriched with Valmiki's active boyhood memories that have erupted into a book. It is a powerful voice against caste violence. The strength of *Joothan* lies in the act of exposing the continuation of caste-based prejudice and power structures of the hegemonic Tyagi community and a belief system that deliberately supported the inhuman practice of untouchability. Hindu myth holds that Brahma has created the universe. Valmiki belongs to the Chura community and he is assigned the responsibility of disposing dead cattle in the village. He breaks the myth of creation and questions the very basis of caste discrimination.

> Being born is not in the control of a person. If it was in one's control, then why would I have been born in a Bhangi household? Those who call themselves the standard-bearers of this country's great cultural heritage, did they decide which home they would be born into? Albeit, they turn to the scriptures to justify their position, the scriptures that establish feudal values instead of promoting' equality and freedom (134).

Valmiki ridicules the so-called Hindu scriptures which have been inherently replete with feudal values meant to serve the religious fundamentalists and hegemonic caste society. Joshua too has the same views about the Hindu myth. He openly questions Brahma, the creator, as to who advised him to create an unequal society. He says, "Who asked you to make a fraudulent creation?" He declares himself to be the universal man. His self-declaration reinforces that he does not belong to any religion. Valmiki breaks caste barriers. His rejection of a community-chosen bride, opposition to his community, traditions, customs and marrying a girl of his own choice indicates his secular stand and a sense of universality. It is synonymous with Joshua's views.

In his school days, Valmiki was assigned to sweep the school yard instead of attending his class. The very assignment is a conspiracy to avoid physical contact with the boy in the class on one hand and to prevent the so-called low castes from learning and assimilating knowledge on the other. Joshua too had almost the same experience in his school where the teacher avoided beating him for he thought that physical contact would amount to pollution. Joshua is optimistic and in that he transforms the teacher's negative attitude into his promising literary career. He appropriately responds to what it can be termed as *Dronaism:*

> Don't boast yourself of mocking at me
> Your comments spared my heart
> Tragic seeds sprouted into finer poetry
> To me, it flourished as a rich gift. (Joshua 221)

In the epic, Dronacharya denies Eklavya archery outright. On the same line, a Tyagi teacher denies schooling to Valmiki. The teacher entrusts him with sweeping work instead of exposing him to education which is a legitimate right of every Indian child. It is one of the techniques employed by the Tyagi teacher. Valmiki's father screams against the assignment and strongly responds. He says, "Who is that teacher, that progeny of Dronacharya, who forces my son to sweep?" (6). Intervention of Valmiki's father is understood as a testimony to the growing consciousness of the entire Dalit community. Valmiki recollects his father's courage and fortitude being displayed with force while confronting the headmaster. Aggressive refusal of 'joothan' by Valmiki's mother is also understood as a rage comparable to that of Durga, the Mother Goddess who is reckoned by the writer as a symbol of fury. He does not find any other suitable metaphor but the 'Hindu goddess'. It does not mean that he is trying to idealize or valorize the Hindu gods who are the representatives of Hindu culture. One of the most powerful moments that capture us is the overturning of a basketful of 'joothan' after Valmiki's mother is humiliated by Sukhdev Singh Tyagi. Valmiki's parents propose such imperatives as the representatives of their entire community. His parents who influenced him a lot have been portrayed as heroic figures in the text. With epic knowledge, Valmiki links the twentieth century casteism with thc onc in the ancient past.

Gandhian philosophy tremendously impacted Joshua. He was attracted by his Non-violence Movement while Valmiki was impacted by Ambedkar's struggles. Joshua is a traditional revolutionary while Valmiki is a modern militant. Though both Joshua and Valmiki differ in their ideological reactions, their caste oppressive lived experiences are the same in Indian society. Joshua cultivates a reformative attitude towards the Hindu society. He virulently denounces the Hindu caste system. But he does not adopt a militant way of resenting the inhuman system of caste. He wrote poetry in highly Sanskritized Telugu as a response to the poetic caliber of Brahmin pundits who claimed that they were the sole authority on Sanskrit knowledge. Valmiki chooses autobiography as a different genre to negate the traditional canon of poetry. Joshua's *Naa Katha* is a counter narration to Sanskrit poetry produced by the elitist sections of his age. "Joshua belonged to the rare class of poets with an intense message of social justice. Like all successful reformers, Joshua, above all, was a humanist who rebelled against injustice, inequality and exploitation" (Rao V).

As a boy, Joshua was contemptuously thrown out by a ticket vender. He became conscious of his place in society although he was too young to realize why it should be that way. He was conscious about the caste society which played havoc in his innocent life. Poverty· was another adverse phenomenon that victimized Joshua. His emotional expletive is evidence of how he as a Dalit poet strongly reacted against the Manu heritage.

> Demon of poverty thrives
> Sucking the poor man's blood
> Four hooded cobra of Hinduism
> That frowns at this very sight. (Joshua 10)

Joshua likens *chaturvarna*[1] with a four hooded cobra that has been hissing for centuries spewing its venom through the institution of caste. It is an open defiance against the Hindu hegemony. Joshua was not a child of the first generation. His father was educated. He was a pastor in a church. Postmodernists are of the view that Valmiki constructs the biological truth in a way he calls people and places by their real names. This is one of the strategies through which Dalit autobiographical writers assure the position of their texts as documentaries of their lived life. In this, Valmiki and Joshua adopt the same strategies. Joshua attributes the problem of caste humiliation to the Hindu social set-up as a whole. Valmiki as a child inherits the spirit of defiance from his parents and starts questioning social inequalities. In the beginning of Joshua's boyhood days, he seems to have spent a care-free life which does not last long. His child-paradise gets entangled with caste and religious ·prejudice. He realizes how the society of his time looked so harsh that he could not freely move with other children. He faced social hindrances everywhere. Joshua's experiences of economic misery and caste humiliation are harsh realities of his life.

In sum, Joshua and Valmiki were the victims of social exclusion and extreme poverty. In their boyhood days, they had unpleasant encounters with their teachers. They were not treated on par with other children in the school. Joshua had a great reverence for his native village. "Even though you forget me, I never forget you" (Joshua n.p). The literary creepers in him were deprived of proper care at his place yet he loved it. This exemplifies his optimism about society and deep affection for his birth place. With Gandhi's social and political inspiration, he enriched his patriotic sense.

Valmiki and Joshua arc brought up in two different socio-cultural milieus and their autobiographies are set in different periods but their literary struggle claims an achieved identity rather than an ascribed one. They successfully overcome the ascribed identity through a literary battle which was relentlessly waged in their respective societies. Both of them were victims of social and religious ostracism. They dreamed of social harmony and equal rights. They vehemently challenged caste-bound social values that shamelessly ascribe their status. Joshua's protesting voice takes on a complaining mode of narration while Valmiki appears rather rebellious because of his different consciousness about the social problems. Though both of them are victims of caste discrimination and poverty, eating of 'joothan' does not seem to be part of Joshua's experience.

However, Joshua and Valmiki try to rise up themselves above their oppressors. They never portray themselves as objects of pity. In Dalit writing, the writer himself or herself is the protagonist. This is one of the significant characteristic features of it. For Joshua, canonical poetry became a potential tool to challenge the caste system of his time. As a poet, he made a significant contribution to Telugu Dalit literature. Valmiki attempts to come out of his 'fractured self' to build a social identity. Honouring Joshua with 'Padma Bhushan' award by upper caste pundits in his time was an eye-wash to his fractured self. But Brahmin pundits who were contemptuous of him did not cease to venerate his poetic talent. Valmiki too made an immense contribution to Hindi Dalit literature by highlighting the plight of Dalits in the post-independence era which is not quite different from that of the pre-independence era. *Joothan* as a vibrant Dalit autobiography successfully made foray into the Indian literary domain. Both Joshua and Valmiki vehemently oppose the very basis of caste discrimination and claim that caste would no longer function as a social force in modern India.

NOTE

1. It is a Sanskrit word. Chatur means four and Varna means 'Groups', means four groups. There were four groups of people Brahmins (Teachers), Kshatriya (Fighters), Vaishya (Traders) and Sudra (Producers), mind it, it is Sudra and not Kshudra (meaning insignificant) or Shudra.

Dissenting Religious Fascism in Enoch's *Munivahanudu*

Munivahanudu, a Telugu Dalit play is written by a renowned Telugu writer, Kolakaluri Enoch. He is the poet, researcher, University teacher, critic and an able administrator. The play focuses on the entry of Thiruppaan Alvar, a devotee of Vishnu, into Sriranganatha temple. Loka Sangaramuni is a priest of the temple. Thiruppan is untouchable by caste. So the priest disallows Thiruppan's entry into the temple. With no foot-prints left on the floor of the temple, Thiruppaan visits Sri Ranganatha using Loka Sarangamuni as his vehicle. Since Srirangamuni was used as a vehicle, Thiruppaan became a Munivahana. The play with mythical and historical attributes argues against social discrimination. It is a great experimental play that disseminates a social message. Besides entertaining the audience/readers, the play gradually creates a kind of consciousness that flows into the Bahujans at the end. Creation of the plot, character portrayal, creation of scenes and diction in the play would show a greater impact on the audience/readers. The play which is crafted in a traditional method is laced with a language full of fragrance. The play was written 40 years ago. But Dalits are yet to gain temple entry. So the story is still relevant to contemporary social situations.

Munivahanudu: A Dalit Play

The play was written in 1976 and it was broadcast as a musical metaphor in All Indian Radio in 1978. Later, it was transformed into a mythical and historical play. Afterwards, it was prescribed in the syllabus for intermediate students from 1985 to 1988. From 2005 onwards, it continued to be prescribed in the M.A syllabus for Dalit literature study in the Department of Telugu, University of Hyderabad. The play received an award from Potti Sriramaulu Telugu University, Hyderabad. This award was considered as equivalent to that of Andhra Pradesh Sahitya Academy. In this play, a lot of research has been done in Sri Venkateswara and Sri Krishna Devaraya universities. Several students have written research papers on it. It has been translated into different Indian languages.

Dr. M.A.K. Sukumar and Dr. Madhurantakam Narendra have translated the play into English. Dr. R. Shisha Shastri has translated it into the Kannada language while Dr. G. Narasimhan in Tamil and Dr. C.P. Reddy in Hindi. The story of the play relates to Sri Ranganatha in Tamil Nadu. Dr. G. Subrahmanyam is of the view that the plot for the play must have been taken from the popular stories and writings associated with the life of Alwars. Several researchers have endorsed his views.

Plot of the Play

The playwright has divided the play into five acts for the convenience of reading. Each act includes important characters such as Thiruppaan Alvar, Sri Ranganatha, Veda Vedya, and Devadatta. Alvars eulogize Vishu by singing their hymns. Among Alvars, twelve were popular. Thiruppaan Alvar is one among them. He belongs to the PAN caste. They were treated as untouchables in society. Story of the play as follows:

In Act I, Thiruppaan goes to the temple to worship Sri Ranganatha. All devotees become spell-bound when he sings in praise of God. Despite his devotion, Loka Sarangamuni, the priest of the temple, does not allow Thiruppan to enter the temple for he belongs to an untouchable community. The priest argues that righteousness will be affected and god will be defiled if Thiruppaan is allowed for worship in the temple.

In Act II, the principal priest of the temple, Loka Sarangamuni goes to the bank of the Kaveri River and fetches sacred water to consecrate Sri Rangeshwara Swamy. Thiruppaan sits in meditation with devotional ecstasy at different places on the bank of the river. The priest apprehends that Thiruppaan would defile the place wherever he sits. The priest also feels that Thiruppaan is defiling places while fetching sacred water from different places to anoint the lord. The priest enrages and hits Thiruppaan with a stone which causes bleeding. The priest feels that Thiruppaan is intentionally defiling the surrounding of the river bank. He tries to inform Thiruppaan through his disciple not to desecrate the places. Pondering the difference between the ordinary stone and the stone lying in the temple, Veda Vedya touches Thiruppaan and cleans the bleeding and bandages the wound. The priest threatens Veda Vedya that he would be disallowed into the temple for physically treating Thiruppaan. The priest also treats Veda Vedya as a *panchama* or untouchable for touching Thiruppaan and warns him that he would not escape from the blows of a stone. Thiruppaan says that his intention is not to do so. But he keeps singing effortlessly in his devotional ecstasy at different places of the river bank. Thiruppaan also feels with devotion that he will be cleansed whenever Loka Sangamuni steps into the river because the priest happens to touch several sacred places in the temple.

In Act III, Loka Saranagamuni brings sacred water every day from the river bank to anoint Sri Ranganatha. Even after knocking with the stone, he fetches sacred water from the river bank the next day also. He forgets that he is bringing sacred water from the place where Thiruppaan meditates. His disciples take notice of all this from a distance. Ved Vedya is also expelled from the temple for physically contacting Thiruppaan; he argues and warns that the priest would also forfeit the eligibility for entry into the temple for he himself violates the temple norms. In response, the priest says he is not responsible for the mistake that is made without his knowledge. But Thiruppaan too meditates in his own fashion. He does not intentionally defile the river banks. Yet, he is knocked and injured. Veda Vedya prohibits the priest's entry into the temple and argues that it is also an equal offence to punish him just for bandaging Thiruppaan's wound. The priest is anguished because he does not take a glimpse of Sri Ranganatha even for a moment. The priest is agonized because Sri Ranganatha neither whole-heartedly accepts the priest's prayer nor shows mercy with his pleasant countenance.

In Act IV, Thiruppaan, engrossed in his meditation, spends his time by singing devotional songs. Bells in Sri Ranganatha's temple reverberate with his songs and the rays of lights travel into the temple. Both Devadatta and Veda Vedya discuss everything. They feel that all the miracles happen because of Thiruppaan's devotional strength that is considered as a strong message from Sri Ranganatha.

Sri Ranganatha appears unhappy and asks Loka Sarangamuni to allow his devotee, Thiruppaan to worship him in the temple. But, the priest is reluctant to do it. The priest says that it will not be possible for him to allow an untouchable to enter the temple. Sri Ranganatha warns that there will not be any defilement as the temple is built for him and he will himself involve in taking care of the entry of his devotee. But, the priest counters the god arguing that the temple is built for the priests and it should be managed as per their norms. The priest also threatens that they (priests) will install any other god from among the three crore gods. Sri Ranganatha enrages over the priest who defies his order and he exudes blood from his eyes. Looking at the sight, the priest says that he cannot behold that unhappy situation. The priest requests the god to appear with his pleasant countenance. To seek a pleasant posture of Sri Ranganatha, Loka Sarangamuni should allow Thiruppaan into the temple. Sri Ranganatha has a long conversation with the priest. The god categorically instructs the priest to carry Thiruppaan on his shoulders for worship. The priest has to do this carefully by avoiding sacrilege if any caused to the temple with Thiruppaan's feet.

In Act V, the priest goes to Thiruppaan who is in deep meditation on the banks of the Kaveri River and carries him to the temple on his shoulders as instructed by Sri Ranganatha. Thiruppaan claims that he is a *panchama* or untouchable. So, no one can physically touch him. The priest replies that he is executing all this as per Sri Ranganatha's instructions. After Thiruppaan is brought into the temple, he worships Sri Ranganatha singing in ecstasy with rapt attention; he gets united with the divine. Thiruppaan appears to all the people through Sri Ranganatha not in the physical form but in the verbal form. Veda Vedya preserves the hymns sung by Thiruppaan and popularizes them.

Theatrical Sculpture

Devotion is an essential aesthetic flavor. An untouchable is chosen as the protagonist and the historical facts are blended with a mythical story. All these three aspects have created a great sculptural diversity in the play. In fact, the play was broadcast as a musical metaphor through all India Radio in Hyderabad with finely tuned music. Verses and songs sung to the context must have produced *rasananda* or a delight of aesthetic flavour to the audience of the day. The audio-play with melodious attributes of poetry creates an interest in the audience who enjoy reading it in an attractive fashion. Sri Rama, Sri Krishna, Sri Ranganatha, Venkateshwara appear to their devotees in different *avatars* or incarnations. When Sri Ranganatha, Thiruppaan, and Loka Sangamuni are united with the divine, Sanskrit expressions loaded with phonetic orientation that release from their mouths look rich in relevance. Sanskrit is considered as a divine language. The playwright has chosen the language of this kind. Descriptions in the play carry a wider connotation. He depicts in a way that Thiruppaan speaks while sitting in a lotus posture.

The sea looks black and tranquil when it is viewed from a distance. Sri Ranganatha's body has a blue complexion like that of Sri Krishna. Though Thiruppaan is not allowed into the temple for he is an untouchable, he speaks out against it. Those who are desirous of finding out the depth of the sea, they only can hear the boisterousness of it. Then, they will come to know whether its original colour is black or white. The same is suggested in acts IV and V.

(Kaveshu Natakam ramyam natakeshu shakusthala Tatrapi Chathurdonka, tatra sloka chatustayam)

Act IV is signified in the conventional plays. The same convention is carried into this play also. In this Act, they have the god who directly speaks to the priest. God speaks on behalf of the devotee whose entry is prohibited. God facilitates to carry his devotee on the shoulders of the priest who disallows the entry of an untouchable into the temple. It is depicted in a way that the entire temple itself is filled with divine efficacy. Sri Ranganatha, describes Thiruppaan as a '*nirmalimanamurthy*'[1] or a serene and unprejudiced personality. Thiruppaan is a personified devotee who conquers *Arishadvargas*[2] *or* the six passions of mind or enemies of desire and waits with the serene mind for worship. Sri Ranganatha queries as to why untouchability is attributed to such a person. The portrayal of Thiruppaan, who is engrossed in Sri Ranganatha's devotion while sitting on the shoulders of Loka Sarangamuni, reminds us of the graphics shown in our day-today movies. This testifies to the playwright's great ideas and talent. The writer depicts that each part of Thiruppaan, such as head, thorax, is engrossed in Sri Ranganatha; Thiruppaan's physical weight on Loka Sarangamuni's shoulders gradually diminishes. Though Thiruppan is united in an inverted position into Sri Ranganatha, the eyes of the devotee get united into God's feet. In Hindu religion, A cult of worshipping god's feet is highly signified. He brings this practice into his play that testifies to his writing skill.

The playwright has Thiruppaan speak out on many occasions. He displays his cosmic form through the creation of pleasure celebration, composition of verses to suit the occasion, description of god and the form of incarnation. Readers become ecstatic with the playwright's style of employing adjectives in Sanskritised words. He exhibits a finer craft of wording in each nomenclature that strikes each different incarnation of Vishnu. Given these descriptions, the play clearly informs that Sri Vishnu incarnates as Sri Rama, Sri Krishna, Sri Venkateshwara and Sri Ranganatha. Contextually language style exemplifies the rich sculpture in this play.

Protagonist, the Essential Aesthetic Flavour

Thiruppaan is the protagonist who plays a key part in the play. Loka Sarangamuni who is the main priest of the temple is a villain. The essence of all orthodox priests in the world is unified into Loka Sarangamuni. Entry into the temple is not just an aspiration of Thiruppaan alone. It is a collective ambition of the untouchable millions. The Hindu religious texts proclaim that God has created the *chaturvarna* system based not on birth but on one's deeds- the *gunadarma*. "In this play, Thiruppaan secures a place in the heart of Sri Ranganatha because of his deeds not because of his birth" (Enoch 95).

Here, the playwright accepts *karma* theory. There are some debatable points as to whether Dalit literature would believe in the existence of God. D.S. Basheer, a research scholar suggests that ' 'it is a popular play which is loaded with social consciousness and the playwright is endowed with progressive thoughts' ' (145). By the time the play was produced, there was no Dalit philosophy in place as strong as it is today. However, a desire for the Harijan upliftment was reflected in several writings. Apart from various arguments, it is the responsibility of a writer to produce a play with an integration of a mythical theme. In the same way, the writer has to clearly reveal his/her perspective. It is the writer's progressive outlook that draws Thiruppaan and Loka Sarangamuni as representatives of the two different ideologies. This could be the main reason for the *Harijans* to be part of reformation movement with an aim to end social discrimination. This would also bring a change to some extent. The playwright artistically foresees a social change through the play. The main objective of the play is not to support *karma* theory nor institutionalize the existence of God. This is not the outlook of the playwright either. For more knowledge, one should read other creative works and criticism produced by the writer.

The protagonist in the play shows enthusiasm in sacrificing his life for the cause of social change. He displays his impeccable devotion to God. Enthusiasm blended with a 'constant level of emotion' is termed as a heroic aesthetic essence. This enthusiasm is manifested through devotion. There are various *veeras* such as *dayaveera*, *dharmaveera*, *danaveera*, *thyagaveera* etc. which can be manifested in many ways.

In the words of Pothukuchi Subramanya Sastri: "Bhagavad Guna shravanam dwaramanovrutthulu uddipitamainappudu Bhagavadakaramtho samleenam aye chittini bhakthi."

God's message continues to flash into one's mind. A person is desirous to be united with God, nothing else. Such desire is called *bhakti* or devotion which is considered as a part of romance. But, it is not considered as a part of *veera rasa or* emotion of heroism. It is an experimental work with a plot being shaped into a mythical and historical play for aesthetic flavor. It is much popularized as being compounded with the social benefit.

"*Vasthuvulu natakamani taruvatha adi prayojanakari ayite lakshana paramarsha awashya karthavyam*" (Enoch 114). It indicates that the aims should be tailored to the elements of the play. Adhering to the theatrical features in the play, the reference of prologue is auspiciously depicted.

> *Sriyuthudu shantachittudu shistarakshakundu*
> *Dushta shikshana dharmamandithundu*
> *Loka Sarangamuni vahana karundu*
> *Vishnu devundu mimmu deevinch gaka*! (Enoch 57)

Sri Mahavishnu is affluent. Laxmi prefers to stay with him. He has a tranquil mind. So he keeps his mind peaceful. He punishes the bad people, protects the good ones and uplifts the virtue. He is so generous that a Dalit can be carried on the shoulders of a priest and performs worship. May Mahavishnu protect you.

The playwright is a master of ceremonies, who speaks out the above lines auspiciously. Though there is a depiction of the spring season, it does not give any aesthetic flavour. G. Balasubramaniam says, "Thirupaan emerges as a sprout from the stumped Dalit community". He aptly comments that lower castes would get good times. The playwright effectively uses Vaishnava tradition in his depiction. Because of the fair and impeccable meditation of Thiruppaan on the banks of the Kaveri River, the temple bells continuously keep ringing. Sri Chary says, "It is a weapon drawn into malfeasance". Malicious feelings and untouchability grounded in Lok Sarangapani look like demons; when they get removed, man's feelings become as sacred as the god. This is the hidden meaning of the ringing bells. Thiruppaan is engrossed in austere meditation on the banks of the Kaveri River. It is perceived from the discussion between Veda Vedya and Devadatta. The playwright powerfully depicts this situation.

The idea of the playwright might be that the effect of Thiruppaan's meditation would make the temple precincts divine somewhere else. It is because unconsciously, Thiruppaan sits in meditation at different places from where the priest takes *theertham* or sacred water. But, the priest considers Thiruppaan as mentally retorted. The priest also presumes that Thiruppaan is intentionally defiling the river water. He knows nothing about it. In the same way, the priest also unconsciously fetches water from the place where Thiruppaan is in deep meditation. It is not that Thiruppaan is already defiled when he is carried on the shoulders of the priest. In the same way, we cannot say that untouchability and defilement have disappeared from Thiruppaan. It is an apt comment made by Chary that "Demonic feelings of the priest are gone and divine attributes are restored".

Alvars--Thiruppaan Alvar

We understand that Alvars wrote nearly four thousand hymns and sang them. The hymns are called *Nayilara*

Divyarabhanda or *Dravida Vedam* altogether (Palavancha Thirumala Gudimella Venkata Lakshmi Narasimha Charyulu, 1994-11). Twelve people have written hymns and sung them. They are known as *pan iddaru* Alvars. Thiruppaan Alvar is one among them. Thiru means 'shri' while 'paan' indicates their community. Alvar means 'those immersed in godliness', mines of knowledge, protectors. The name of Alvars became popular as protectors of the people and they shared devotional knowledge with those who believed in Vishnu. Thiruppaan Alvar hailed from Urayur in Tamil Nadu. He is a historic person who belonged to 8th century. He was also known as Paanar, Munivahana, Yogivahana and Kavishwera (Ayam Hitam Nateswara Sarma, 1992-vi). The people of Paan community, who were music lovers, became popular in playing *veena* or a traditional musical instrument and singing psalms, and received honours from the royal courts. They were companions of *Devadasis* in Vaishnava temples. There was a drastic change in social life as popularity of the artists steadily declined. With the passage of time, all of them began to be treated as untouchables.

Social Dimensions

Kolakaluri Enoch has deployed a limited number of characters that include four human characters and one divine character. Depicting Veda Vedya and Devadatta as conflicting and controversial characters to represent different ideologies in Hindu religion, the playwright has customizes Devadatta as a transformed character who finally realizes a reality from Veda Vedya's arguments. Veda Vedya is depicted as a representative of the fair hearted thinkers even among the orthodox Hindus. Thus the playwright heralds a healthy change in society. Describing the nature of Thiruppaan, the playwright says: "He is a unified form of racial anguish that has not visited God for generations. Thiruppaan is not just a person but a system" (Enoch 105).

The playwright, who has chosen a mythical plot and integrates it with historical experience, has given an artistic form to a severe problem that has created social inequality, and he has produced the play with a responsibility in order to create awareness towards a casteless society.

The names of Veda Vedya and Devadutta may create confusion during the performance. But, when a reader goes through the play as an audio-play, the names appear to be a little complicated. When we ponder it, we understand that the playwright has created and named the characters with some intent. He represents key words in the play through a character. Veda Vedya argues with Devadatta that Loka Sarangamuni fetches sacred water to anoint Sri Ranganatha without noticing Thiruppaan who is in deep meditation on the banks of the Kaveri River. The priest also unconsciously brings the water. When Veda Vedya explains, Devadatta realizes that he has also got enlightened: "Devadatta! Every human being is the same, just physical differences, in spiritual terms, everyone's the same! You and I are the same! Devadatta is Veda and God is Veda Vedya! In Deva-Veda, the duo's lives are stable!" (Enoch 78).

It is inferred that the playwright has intentionally created characters like Veda Vedya and Devadatta. However, these characters certainly create some confusion in the minds of the readers. Questions can also be raised whether the society portrayed in the play belongs to the 8th century AD or to the 20th century. Good and bad may not emerge in a society overnight. Some of them will undergo a change over a period of time. Economic, political and administrative decisions may have been impacted. These decisions are intended to influence some sections. Despite socio-political cosmetic changes, caste and religion are a potential threat at the ground level. Problems are addressed based on the evolved social system. The playwright depicts how the practice of untouchability has been in place from the time of Thiruppaan and also its impact on the present society. In *Amuktamalyada* written by Sri Devaraya, the story of Maladasari might be that of Thiruppaan.

Maladasari--Thiruppaan Alvars

Sri Krishnadevaraya's Maladasari represents the socio-religious circumstances of his time. The emperor is said to have enforced *chaturvarna* or four-fold system of caste. He delineates *chaturvarna* in verses ranging from 33 to 36 in the Act II of *Amuktamalyada.* Though Thiruppaan Alvar impacts Mala Dasari, the world view of Sri Krishna Devaraya is much different from that of Kolakaluri Enoch. Devotion is sought in different ways from worshipping God to the end of unity with Him. The procedures like *shravanam, sankeerthanam, smaranam, archanam, vandanam, dashyam, sakyam, atma nivedanam* are known as *nava bak this* or nine devotions. The poet depicts *dashya bhakthi* in Vishnu *chitthu, shakya bhakti* in Godadevi, *sankeertana bhakthi* in Maladasari. With a reformative perspective in the act of social transformation, Kolakaluri dramatizes the theme. To write this play, he must have carefully followed the history of Alvars: "There are different sects within the Vaishnavas. Thiruppaan Alvaruni claimed that Sri Krishna Devaraya belonged to the Thenkalai sect with the Alvars. There are about 18 ideological differences between *Vadagali* and *Thenkalai* sects within Srivaishnavam" (Ayam Hitam Nateswara Sarma, 1992, ix-xii).

Each sect has a different devotional path and approach for salvation. *Vadugalai* says that one can try for devotion and salvation without violating the etiquettes of *Varnasrama Dharma* while *Thengalai* claims that "all the people deserve respect in society irrespective of disparities between the low and the high when it is supported with the pleasure of god" (Ayam Hitam Nateswara Sarma, 1992-ix-xii). Though both Sri Krishna Devaraya and Kolakaluri Enoch depict the life of Alvars, but researchers claim that Sri Krishna Devaraya portrays an Alvar from the viewpoint of *Varaha Purana* while Kolakaluri Enoch depicts the life of Thiruppaan Alvar from a progressive perspective. In fact, Sri Krishna Devaraya delineates the story of Mala Dasari[3] within the frame of the chaturvarna or fourfold system of caste.

Pothanna, who conducted research on Kolakaluri Enoch's works, expresses his views on the play that "He (Thiruppaan) possesses a serene mind, sincerity and wholehearted devotion, yet he is worried about the temple entry because he is an untouchable; if he were touchable there would not have been a problem" (34). Pothanna says, "The playwright has written the play to inform the readers about this. "God has no feeling of untouchability. It has evolved only among human beings. It is created by certain dominant orthodox sections. Sri Ranganatha who hears the prayer of Thiruppaan, wishes to fulfill the desire of his child" (Potana 34).

In the words of Balasubramaniam, "The play offers a due recognition to the traditional revolution and even the revolution seeking virtue would be an ideal act". "This play is written to inform qualitatively and artfully as to how untouchability, which is against the spirit of the Vedas, has done so much harm to Indian society and it has caused a hindrance to the unity of nation" (Ramana 135).

He also opines that the play has been shaped into a distinct style with internal outlook on materialism and spiritualism as well. Given the research done on the play and also the views expressed by the critics, it is understood that even after three decades of independence of India, Dalits are still dismissed as untouchables. It is the play which strongly represents this fact.

After reading or watching or listening, the audience would understand the fact and ponder as to how Dalits are treated in society even today. Songs, verses, dialogues enshrined in the play would manifest the playwright's literary caliber in many ways. Above all, it would make the reader think how the theme in the play is developed and treated. Audience would wholeheartedly accept the arguments of the playwright once the play is read, listened or watched through performance. The play is illustrated as a harmonious representation of caste and religious problem" (Rao n.p). The same inspiration is noticed in the epilogue:

> Ee Thiruppan prakashame ilaku migula
> Pilachi Sri Ranganatha Du Velugumatla
> Sarva Samanya Manava Shakthi Pondi
> Praja Prathinidhi Janulu Kapadugaka. (Enoch 109)

Many social aspects connected with the dialogues that take place between the characters in the play need to be viewed from a philosophical perspective. The playwright who recognizes the need to explain more to the readers the advantage and essence of the dialogues is also credited with "Kalavrita" a story known for its strong popularity. The dialogue between the priest and the untouchable is intellectual and artistic (Rao 2007). The dialogue between the two of them reflects a change over the temple system in a way that the priest is not for God but for the priest. On the whole, Kolakaluri Enoch has shaped *Munivahanudu* for the benefit of society with a mythical and historical integration. Though it is forty years since the play was written, Dalits have not yet been allowed to enter temples at many places of India. As long as the social discrimination exists, Dalit plays like Munivahanudu will continue to be written. Such plays are also still necessitated today apart from creating a sense of devotion and self-confidence in the social margins in order to remember the sacrifices made by those who fought against the social evils.

NOTES

1. The god appreciates Thiruppan for his serene mind and elegant personality with true devotion.
2. It is because his devotee conquers six passions of mind. A true devotee is required to fulfil these *arishadvargas*.

Bibliography

Balasubramanniyam. *Prof. Kolakaluri Enoch Shastipurthy Sanmana Sanchika*. Publication, 1999.

_____. *Naataka Shrastaga Enoch.*

Basheer, D.S. *Munivahanudu Natakam- Enoch gari Drukpatham. 1999*.

Bheemanna, Boyi. *Raagavasistam*. Hyderabad: Kalanikethan Prachuranalu, 1959.

Colas, Santiago. What is wrong with Representation? *Testimonio and Democratic Culture in The Real Thing: Testimonial Discourse and Latin America*, ed George M. Gugelberger. Durham: Duke University Press, 1996.

Carroll, David. *Chinua Achebe*. London: Macmillan, 1992.

Coral, A. Walker. 'Evolution of Genres in Latin American Literature'. *The Birth of the Testimonial* (Testimonial Narrative) < https://www.swarthmore.edli/x10953.xml>.

Gnananandakavi. S.T. *Scheduled Kulalu Antaraniva*! Kakinada: Suragali Prachuranalu, 1997.

Gugelberger, G. and M. Kearney. "Voices for the Voiceless: Testimonial Literature in Latin America," *Latin American Perspectives* 18.3 (1991).

Ilaiah, Kancha. *Madiga Arthika Tatwam*. Hyderabad: Ekalavya Prachuranalu, 1996.

_____. *Why I am not a Hindu*, Calcutta: Samya, 2000.

Laban Babu, Talluri, Madigavari Cheritra. Kusumanjali Prachuranalu, 2001.

_____. *Nalladraksha Pandiri*. Secunderabad: Manasa Prachuranalu, 2002.

_____. *Virgin Karaneeyam*. Rajahmundry: Manasa Prachuranalu, 2003.

_____. *Kotta Gabbilam*, Rajamandri: Manasa Prachuranalu, 1998.

Lakshmaiah, Mallepally, ed. *Jambava Puranam*. Hyderabad: Janapada Parishodhana, 1997.

Jagannatham, Nomulakanti. *Arundathi Devi Charitramu*. Hyderabad: Vaidika Grantha Prachara Mandali Prachuranalu, 1968.

Joshua, Gurram. *Naakatha*, vol. iii. Hyderabad: Navayuga Publishing House, 2006.

_____. *Gabbilam.* Vijayawada: Jashua Foundation, 1996.

_____. *Gabbilam*, Trans. K. Madhav Rao. Hyderabad: Jashua Foundation, 1998.

Madhusudhana Saraswathi Bhakthi Rasayanam U.

Murthy, B.B.S. *Dalita Katha Manjari.* Rajahmundry: Triveni Printers,1992.

Nannaiah. *Andhra Mahabharatam*. Tirupati: Thirupathi Devasthanam Publications, 1996.

Narsaiah, Lakhshmi, *Dalita Sahityam, Tatvika Bhoomika*. Hyderabad: Dalita Sana Prachuranalu, 1999.

Potana. *Acyarya Kolakaluri Enoch Plays and Dramas*. 1994.

Rajasekhar, V.T. *The Black Untouchables in India*. Atlanta Clarity Press, 1932.

Reddy, K. Indrasena. *The Novels of Achebe and Ngugi.* New Delhi: Prestige, 1994.

Rama Rao Bonigala. *Mala-Madiga prachina Charitra.* Kakinada: Prashanta Offset Printers, 1998.

Rama Rao, Bonigala. *Adiguruvu Acharya Chandala.* Tenali: Swiya Publications, 2005.

_. *Adiguruvu Acharya Chandala*. Tenali: Sweeya Publications, 2005.

Ramana. *The undying beat of the Dappu: How a traditional drum signifies dignity, revolution for the Madiga community.*

_____. *Manava Jeevana Vedanalu-Enoch Natakalu.* 1999.

Seetharama Charyulu, Bavujanapally. *Shabda Ratnakaram*, (A Dictionary of Telugu Language). The Madras School Book and Vernacularly, 1937.

Shyamala, Gogu, ed. 'Tataki.' Nalla Regadi *Sallu: Madiga Ukulala Adolla Kathalu.* Hyderabad: Mysamma Sabbanda, 2006.

Subba Chary, Pulikonda, ed. Kolanupaka Nulaka Chandaiah la Adi Jambava Mahapuranam. Kuppam: Dravida Univ., 2008.

Subhadra, Jupaka, ed. 'Manyem', *Nallaregadi Sallu: Madiga Ukulala Adolla Kathalu.* Hyderabad: Mysamma Maisamma Sabbanda, 2006.

Subramanya Sastri, *Pothukuchi. Prathama Swasam-Venkateswara Rao, Darla. Pidibakuluga Mare Poolu Enoch Vakkayalu*. Vyasam, Saranga, 2014.

Sudhakar, Yendluri. *Virgin Karaneeyam*. Rajahmundry: Manasa Prachuranalu, 2003.

_____. *Mallamoggala Godugu Madiga Kathalu*. Hyderabad: Dandora Prachuranalu, 1999.

Sunder Raju, Nagappa gari. *Madiga Chaitannyam*. Hyderabad: Madika Sahitya Vedika Prachuranalu, 1997.

_____. *Chandala Chatimpu*. Hyderabad: Madika Sahitya Vedika Prachuranalu, 1996.

Valmiki, Omprakash. *Joothan.* Trans. Arun Prabha Mukerjee. New Delhi: Popular Prakashan, 2003.

Varalaxmi, P. "Literature and Social Change: Chinua Achebe's *Things Fall Apart*," *African Literature Today* ed. R.K. Dhawan, New Delhi: Prestige Books, 1994.

Vijaya Bharathi, B. *Puranalu Kula Vyavastha*. Hyderabad: Hyderabad Book Press, 2001.

Vyakya, Sadhana Grantahmandali Publication, Tenali.

Web Citations

"Culture-Madiga". https://en.wikipedia.org/wiki/Madiga

"Dalit Goddess-Madiga". https://en.wikipedia.org/wiki/Madiga

"Origins – Madiga". https://en.wikipedia.org/wiki/Madiga

"Sanskrit Roots-Madiga". https://en.wikipedia.org/wiki/Madiga